"This book is a great general-purpose resource of practical and visual effects for the beginning filmmaker."

— Eric Chauvin, visual effects artist for *The Empire Strikes Back, War of the Worlds, Lost, Alias* and *The X-Files*

"This book shows how easy it can be to make Hollywood-style effects. If you're looking to increase the production value of your independent films or even your home movies, this is the book for you."

— Per Holmes, award-winning music producer and music video director

"This book is a tremendous resource for all filmmakers. This book contains so much information you'll constantly be going back for more."

— Andrew Kramer, visual effects artist, teacher and consultant

"With a broad look at special and visual effects that can really increase the visual appeal and power of ultra-low budget films, *Special Effects* is a must-own effects primer for low-budget filmmakers the world over!"

— Jeremy Hanke, editor. *Microfilmmaker Magazine* (www.microfilmmaker.com)

"An interesting look at special effects techniques, both old and new."

— Simon Jones, editor, FXHome, creator of visual effects software

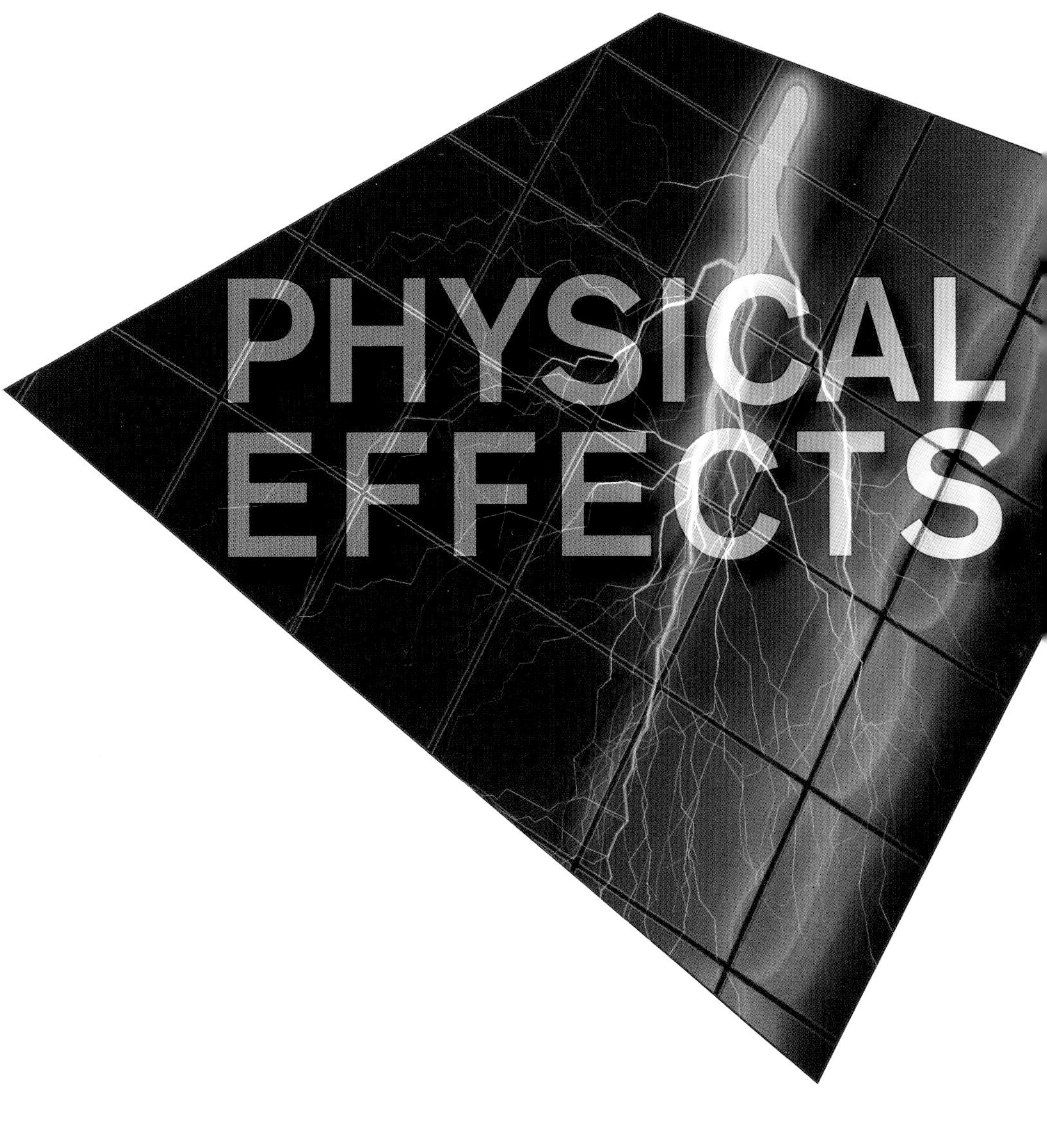
PHYSICAL
EFFECTS

SECTION 1

SMOKE AND DRY ICE MACHINES

There are several types of situations that call for smoke or fog. They can help you create a certain mood, add depth to a scene or create the effect of something on fire. The two most common ways to create fog and smoke are with a **smoke machine** or a **dry ice machine**. The dry ice machine is used more in theatrical productions, and creates smoke that tends to hang in the air and float across the floor better than a smoke machine. However, the smoke machine can create more smoke at a much faster rate, which can be a real advantage on a movie set. Smoke machines can also be very small and portable. All you need is an electrical outlet to plug into and a bottle of good smoke machine fluid, also called **Fog Juice** or **Fog Fluid**. Once the smoke machine has had time to heat up and has been filled with fluid, you are ready to go.

As of this writing, I found quite a few smoke machines for sale on the Internet for between $39 and $100. A bottle of **Fog Juice** cost about $6. This is a very inexpensive item considering the many types of effects it can create for you.

One advantage of dry ice machines are that they create a "low-laying fog" that could be very useful in some situations. They are not as portable or as fast as smoke machines, but they definitely have their place in the effects business. There are several sites on the Internet that will teach you how to build your own dry-ice machine and I also found several companies that were selling them. They were much more expensive than the smoke machines, and you will need access to "dry ice" as well.

** This section includes information from Likeastory.com*

SMOKE MACHINES

- Creates more smoke at a faster rate than dry-ice machines
- Small and portable
- Fairly inexpensive

DRY-ICE MACHINES

- Creates smoke that tends to float across the floor
- Slower than smoke machines
- Not easily portable
- More expensive than smoke machines
- Requires "dry ice" which can be dangerous if not handled properly

SNOW

Snow can be artificially made in several ways. Some movies have used shaved ice and painted corn flakes. The white corn flakes make good "falling snow" and also add a crunch to your characters walking.

For snowdrifts, you can use papier-mâché that has been painted white. For shots that are far away, you can use white bed sheets that are spread out, cotton or shaving cream.

Most hobby shops sell fake snow that can work very well, and there are also fake snow sprays that you can buy to "frost the windows." These are called **Snow Spray** and **Spray-On Ice**.

If the set is small, you can grind up PVC pipe and use the shavings as snow. Crushed ice also works well.

If these ideas don't work for your situation, there are other options available. The following ideas are a little more expensive, but I wanted to include them anyway.

A store called **Green Set** in North Hollywood, CA., offers boxes of shaved plastic. They come in three different sizes — fine, medium and coarse. A thirty-pound box costs $100 and covers an area 10′ x 10′. If you need to cover a larger area, they also offer a **Snow Blanket** that is made of white batting. This comes in a roll 4 ½′ x 75′ for $100 or 6′ x 75′ for $150. You could also mix a little shaved plastic snow with the snow blanket to create a more realistic scene. The phone number for **Green Set** is (818) 764-1231 and their website is **www.greenset.com**.

Another option for white, fluffy snow is **Sno Foam**. This takes a little more effort than the other ideas, as you will need a gallon or more of **Sno Foam**, a **Sno Foam** generator, a garden hose and an air compressor. **Sno Foam** comes as a concentrate, and you end up blowing it all over your set. One gallon of **Sno Foam** costs $73.50 and will cover an average-sized front yard. A company called **Tri-Ess** sells the **Sno Foam** and also rents the **Sno Foam** generator for $50 a day. They are located in Burbank, CA, and their phone number is (818) 848-7838. Check out their website at **www.tri-esssciences.com**.

** This section includes information from Likeastory.com*

This is a miniature forest we created as a background for some shots. However, the scene called for a forest covered in snow.

With the help of a can of **Fake Snow**, our green forest soon became a winter wonderland.

Here is how our forest looked for the final shot.

Another scene called for a snow-frosted window. Since there was no natural snow available, we had to improvise.

With some more help from our can of **Fake Snow**, the window is "frosted" in no time.

Here is how our window looked for the final shot.

SECTION 3

RAIN

There are a few different ways to create a rain effect. One way is to use one or more sprinklers. You can hide them in a tree, on a roof, on a ladder or just about any other place you can think of. The trick is to have the water spray up into the air, and then fall down naturally. If you set the sprinklers so they shoot the water straight down, this will look very unnatural and will affect the realism of the shot. This might work if you are shooting the water onto the outside of a window, but otherwise, you should always have the water spraying up in the air and then falling down.

Another way is to create an inexpensive rainbar. Hollywood professionals use rainbars to create the effect of rain for major motion pictures. While they use professional equipment, you can create a simple version of the rainbar, which can be very effective. For the example on the following pages, we used a six-foot piece of ¾ inch **PVC pipe**. You can make yours longer or shorter depending on your needs. Here is what you will need:

- A piece of ¾ inch **PVC pipe**, long enough to meet your needs. One end should have a bell housing
- Marker, pen or pencil
- Drill and drill bits
- Can of PVC cement
- ¾ inch PVC end cap
- ¾ inch PVC garden hose adapter
- Clamp and ladder, or another way to secure the rainbar
- Garden hose connected to a water faucet

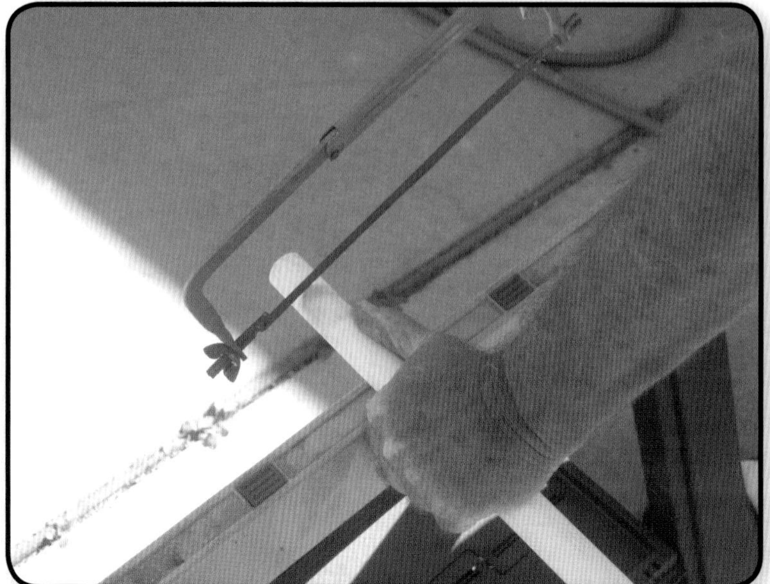

Cut the **PVC pipe** to your desired length. In the example above, we used a ¾ inch six-foot-long piece.

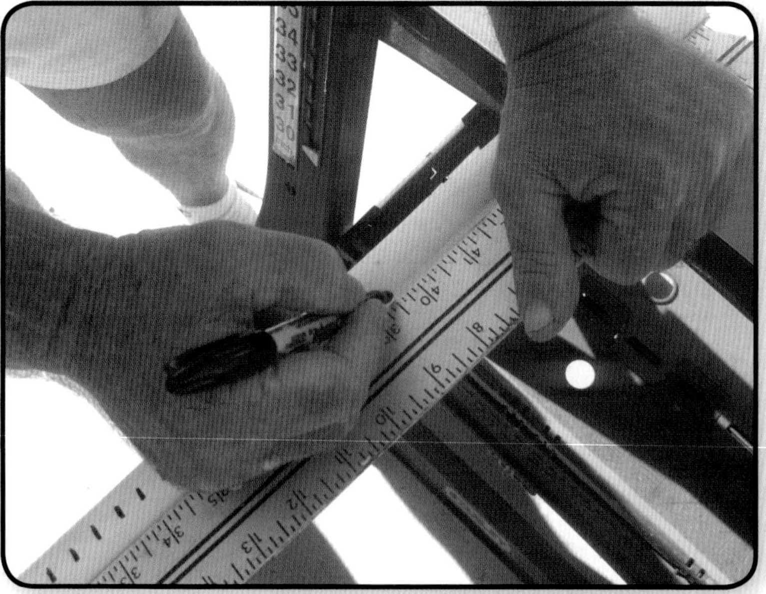

Make a mark every ½ inch down the top of the **PVC pipe**.

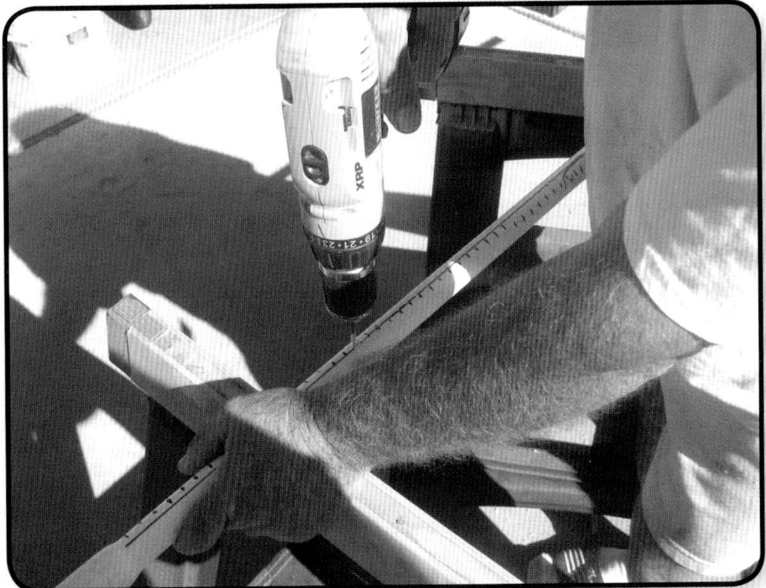

Using a small drill bit, drill a hole on each mark. The reason you should start off with a small hole first is because you can always make them bigger if you need more water to come out.

Cover the end of the **PVC pipe** without the bell housing with **PVC cement**.

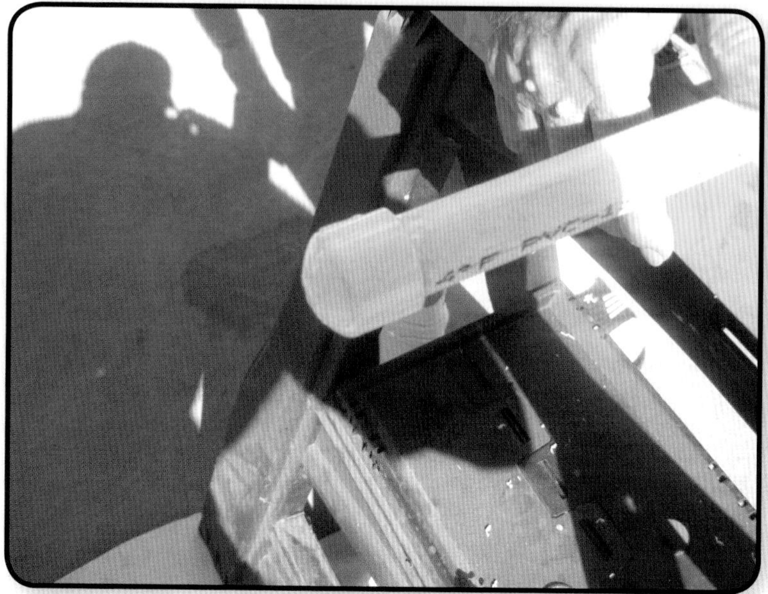

Securely attach the **PVC** end cap over the end of the **PVC pipe** and cement.

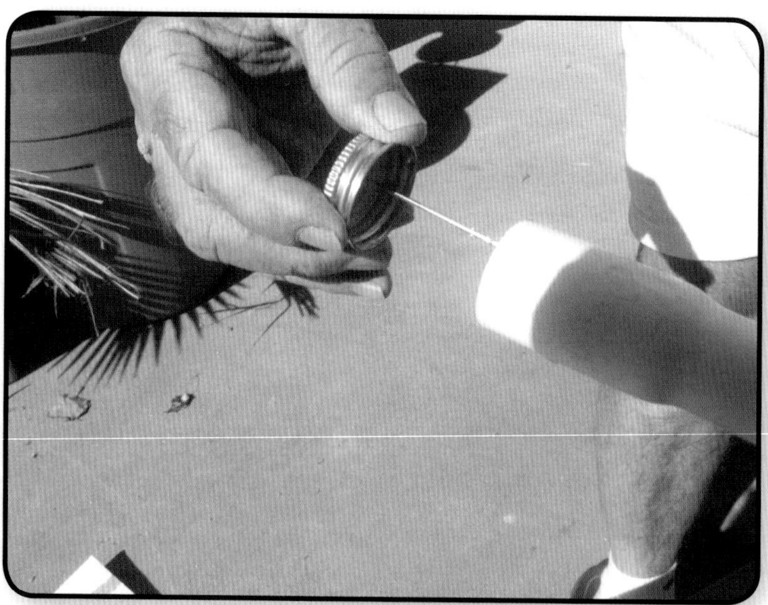

Coat the inside of the bell housing with **PVC cement**.

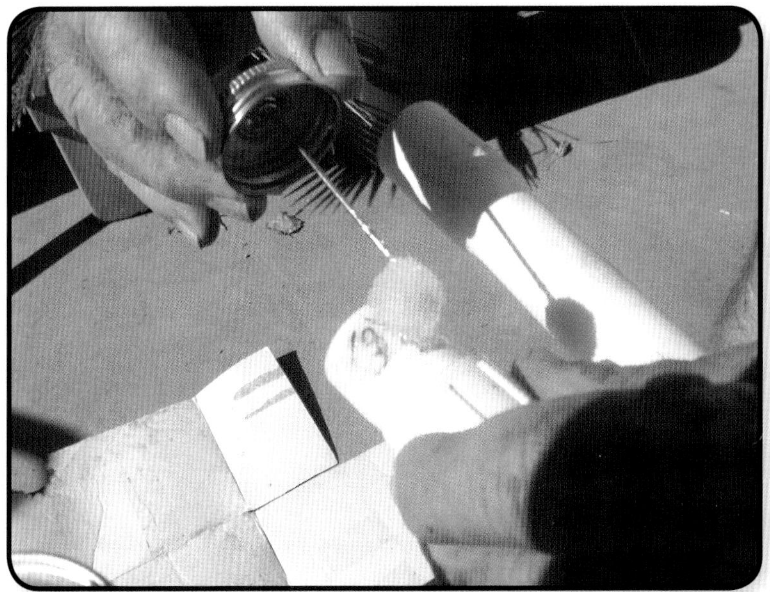

Cover the end of the **PVC** garden hose adapter with **PVC cement**.

Securely insert the **PVC** garden hose adapter into the bell housing on the **PVC pipe**. If the **PVC pipe** you are using doesn't have a bell housing, you can use a ¾-inch **PVC** coupling instead.

Attach a garden hose to the **PVC** garden hose adapter and then secure the rainbar to the top of your ladder with a clamp. If the rainbar is too long to be supported by one ladder, you can use a clamp and ladder on each end of the rainbar for support.

You might need to place a small wooden block under the rainbar for support.

SECTION 4

FAKE GLASS

Some shots call for breaking some type of glass. What do you do if you need to smash a glass bottle or throw a punch through a window? This can be very dangerous, so what is a low-budget independent filmmaker supposed to do? If you need a breakaway bottle, glass or plate, you can buy these from **Premier Studio Equipment**. Their products are made of a special plastic that breaks just like glass. They average about $25 each.

Premier Studio Equipment
www.premierstudioequipment.com
(909) 427-8591

If you need to break a window, then you need a company that can make custom breakaway glass windows. **Alfonso's Breakaway Glass Inc.** has provided breakaway glass for many movies and can create custom pieces for your next production.

Alfonso's Breakaway Glass Inc.
www.alfonsosbreakawayglass.com
(818) 768-7402

SECTION 5

PEOPLE DISAPPEARING

This is a very easy effect to create, but it can be extremely effective. One minute a person is walking through a shot, and then suddenly he is gone... vanished!

The trick to this effect is that you need to keep the camera perfectly still throughout the entire shot. The best way to do this is with a camera tripod. You can also set the camera on a sturdy surface, but if the camera moves even a little bit, it will ruin the effect.

First, record someone sitting or walking. Next, pause the camera (make sure the camera does not move at all). Have the person exit out of the scene. Start recording again.... That's it! When you play it back, it will seem as if your actor has disappeared.

Please see the example on the next page.

REC
PAUSE
REC
PAUSE
REC
PAUSE

SECTION 6

PROP GUNS

Some movies call for a good shootout, or the need for realistic looking guns. The guns made by **Airsoft** (**www.airsoftus.com**) are realistic looking and several of them offer what **Airsoft** calls "Gas Blowback." The Blowback effect is a simulation of the slide action of a real gun. The slide cycles back and forth with each shot, simulating a real gun. When gun flashes are added with a computer (check out the digital section of this book for information on this), the final results can be extremely realistic. **Airsoft** also makes guns without the Blowback feature. They make all types of guns including rifles, pistols and silencers. They offer such a huge selection of weapons that there is a good chance you will find what you are looking for. The normal guns range in price from about $35 to $100. The Gas Blowback guns start around $150. However, we have found most of the **Airsoft** guns for sale at indoor swap meets and auctions for about half that price.

The Blowback guns require you to buy a special gas (**Green Gas**) to create the Blowback effect. Cans of **Green Gas** range in price from $5 to $35.

Several of the guns also come with a removable clip. You can insert it into the gun and also "pop" it out, just like a real gun. Several of the guns can also be "cocked" by pulling back the top slide. All of these features just add to the realism. Each of the guns can work in different ways, so make sure you ask a lot of questions when you buy your gun, to make sure it will do what you want it to.

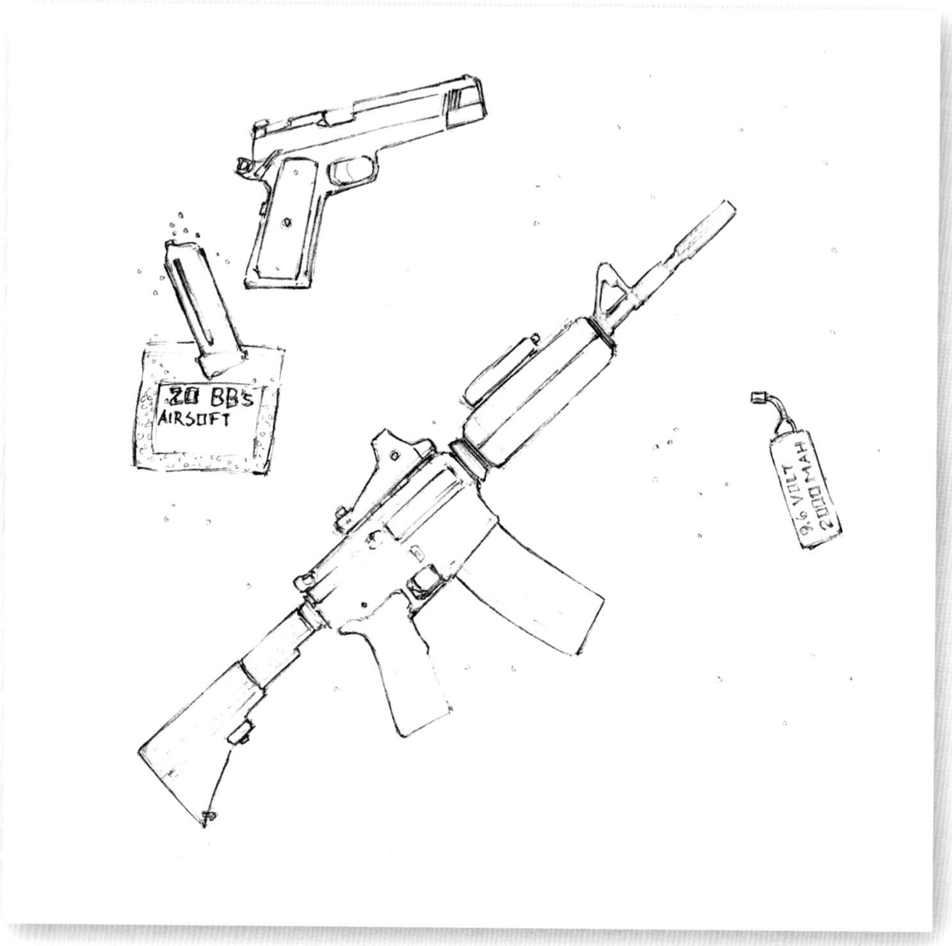
20 BB's
AIRSOFT
9.6 VOLT
2000 MAH

Airsoft pistols look very realistic.

Some **Airsoft** pistols have removable clips, which add to the realism.

Some **Airsoft** pistols have a realistic slide action. This allows the gun to be "cocked."

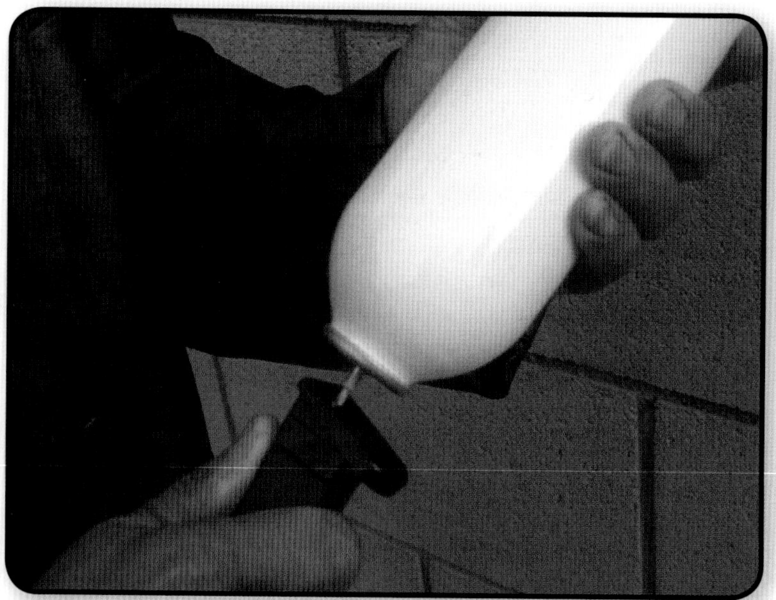

This picture shows the gun clip being filled with **Green Gas**.

SECTION 7

BULLET HITS: PAINTBALL SHOTS

A very realistic way to simulate bullet hits is with "special" Paintball shots. They are small plastic balls that you fire from a Paintball gun. You can buy them from **Roger George Rentals** in Van Nuys, CA. They will fit most standard paintball guns, but you will want to try one out first before you buy a lot of them, just to make sure they fit your gun. Here is the contact information for Roger George Rentals:

Roger George Rentals
Van Nuys, CA
(818) 994-3049
www.hollywired.net/rogergeorge

The Paintball shots are called **Sweeney Balls**. You can buy them as blanks or you can buy them pre-made. The blank shots cost .35 cents each. They come as two plastic halves. You have to fill them yourself, and then glue them together. Most of the pre-made shots cost $1.25 each. They come pre-filled and already glued together. They can come filled with fuller's earth (for shots hitting the ground), black dust powder, red dust powder or white dust powder. You can also buy Sweeney Balls filled with **Zirconium**. These shots tend to spark when you fire them at metal objects. They have to be fired a certain way to look realistic, but the people at Roger George Rentals can teach you how to do this. The Zirconium shots cost $1.50 each. I have tried several of the Sweeney Balls, and the black dust hits seem to work the best. I use them for almost all of my shots.

As with anything, Paintball guns and Sweeney Balls can be very dangerous if they are not used with extreme caution, and used in the way that they were intended. Please read the instructions and warnings that come included with your Paintball equipment, and always practice "Safety First".

** This section includes information from Likeastory.com*

The Paintball gun we use is the ACI F4 Illustrator.

This picture shows several different colors of **Sweeney Balls**. It also shows what you need to make them yourself — the empty plastic halves, **Q-tips** and **IPS "Weld-On" Cement**.

This picture shows two **Bullet Hits** striking a table.

This picture shows several **Bullet Hits** striking a table.

SECTION 8

MODELS AND MINIATURES

Some shots are too costly to create. They might require a building, a mountain or a whole city block. They might portray a train falling off its tracks or a flash flood raging through city streets. You might need to show an avalanche with huge rocks rolling down a mountain or any number of scenarios. Since most of these scenes would be too costly or dangerous to create, realistic simulations can be done with miniatures and models. We aren't going to explain how to build a city or make a mountain fall down, but we are going to give a few suggestions and hopefully point out where to find help. Models and miniatures can be a huge advantage to the beginning filmmaker.

One of the best places to find supplies and to receive help is a local hobby store. Most good hobby shops will have an extensive supply of trees, foliage, buildings and scenery. They should also have books available on miniatures and models, both the creation and setup. There are also a lot of books on model trains, which can include excellent step-by-step instructions for creating all types of scenes. They can teach you how to create mountains, bridges, lakes, rivers, snow scenes, city scenes, and the list goes on. Along with the books and supplies, the people that work at or frequent these shops can also be a wealth of information and help.

The library is also a good place to search. They can provide books that range from basic art to advanced model making.

One of the most important things to remember when dealing with models and miniatures is that the smallest details need to be taken care of. If you really want to "sell a shot" and make it believable, don't forget the small details. For example, if you're building a city street, don't forget things like manhole covers, streetlights, power lines, mailboxes and newspaper stands. It's the smallest details that make the biggest difference.

Whatever type of scene you are trying to recreate, you should visit actual locations and take lots of pictures. These pictures will be your reference guides for your models and miniatures, and help you to remember all of the smallest details.

Lighting can also help create realism. Once you build your miniature set, you can use lights to add shadows, darken or lighten the scene, add texture, or set the mood. Once you have the set done and have painstakingly re-created all of the tiniest details, the lighting is the final step. Experiment with different lights at different angles until you find the exact look you are searching for.

You can also replace the glass in the **Glass Shot** with your model or miniature. Just place your model on a stand a few feet in front of the camera. Make sure your actors and other background elements are much further back behind your model. Please see the example below.

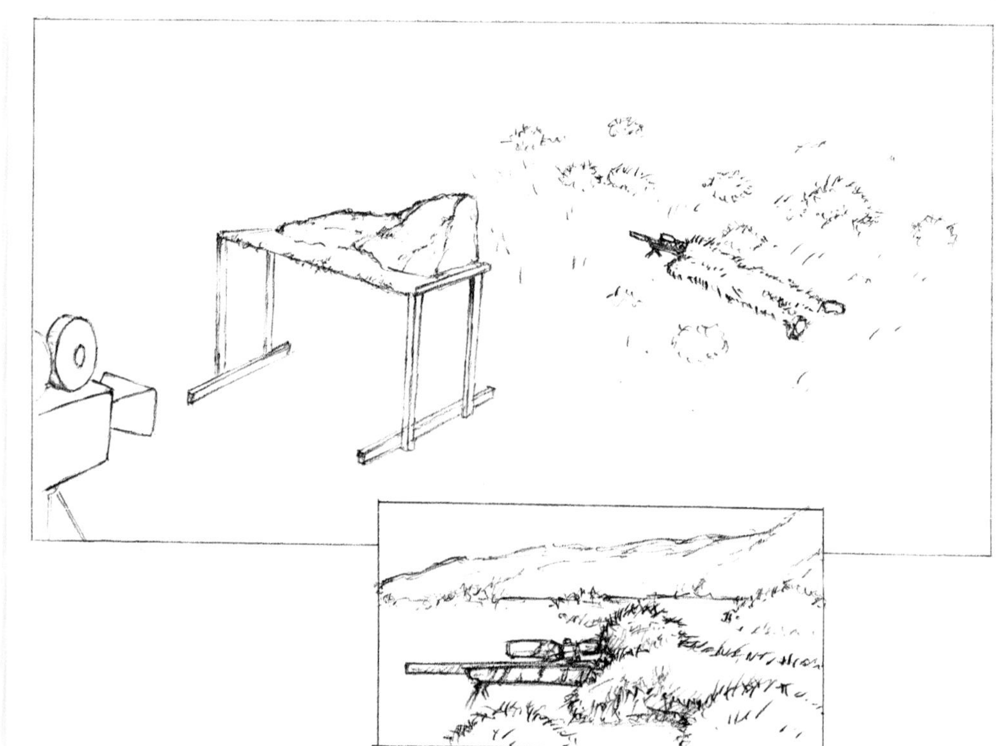

An average house in an average neighborhood.

Another picture of the same house.

Maybe this isn't your average house.

This miniature house has a lot of small details, which really helps to create the illusion.

SECTION 9

STAGE BLOOD

Some scenes need a little blood. What would a car crash or emergency operation be without some blood? **Stage Blood** comes in all different sizes, according to your needs. You can buy small bottles with as little as one ounce or you can buy it by the gallon. Stage Blood also comes in different colors and textures. **Star Light and Magic** sells realistic looking imitation blood to cover most of your needs. They sell regular red blood, green oozing alien blood and even blood thickening powder. Just add a small amount of the thickening powder to your Stage Blood to create extra thick, congealed blood. There are dozens of companies that sell Stage Blood and they can be found with a simple internet search. Below is the contact information for Star Light and Magic.

Star Light and Magic
www.starmgc.com
(800) 275-4800

When buying **Stage Blood**, make sure you understand exactly what you are purchasing. Is it for external use only? Is it easily washed out of clothes and fabrics? Is it flavored? Are there any harmful side effects? Ask a lot of questions before buying and make sure you feel confident with the product.

SECTION 10

ARROW HITTING AN OBJECT

Have you ever wanted to be **Robin Hood**? Have you ever dreamed of shooting an arrow and hitting any target you aimed for? Now, with the help of Special FX, you can. This is really a simple trick, and if it is done correctly, it can be very effective. First, film a close-up shot of your actor firing an arrow off-screen. Next, secure the arrow into whatever you were shooting at. If it was a tree, stick the arrow securely into the tree. If it was a fence, then stick the arrow securely into the fence. Next, tie a long piece of string, thread or fishing line onto the end of the arrow. It must be the kind that cannot easily be seen. It must also be long enough so that someone can hold the end of it and not be seen by the camera. Next, have someone pull the string down which will cause the end of the arrow to arc down. Start recording on your camera, and let go of the string. The end of the arrow will fly up and down repeatedly. Add the sound effect of an arrow striking an object and you are done. The sound effect is very important and is essential to creating the illusion. Please see the example on the next page.

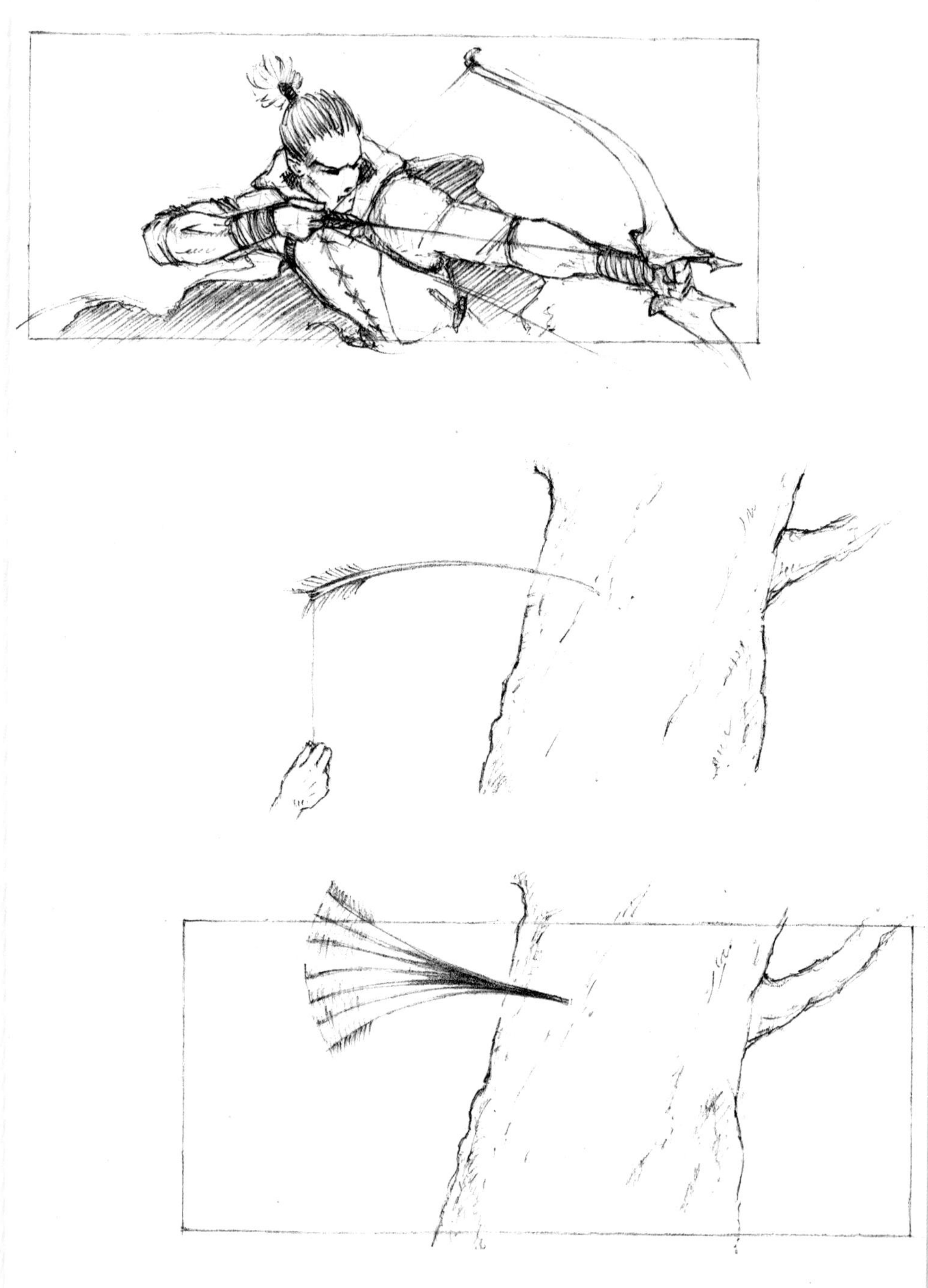

DIGITAL
EFFECTS

SECTION 11

DIGITAL SOFTWARE

With the advances of technology, the tools of professional filmmakers are now available to the beginner and independent filmmakers. You can now buy video editing, sound editing, compositing, painting, titling, 3D creation and a host of other software and hardware packages for your home computer. You can now shoot your movies on high-quality digital cameras and perform all of your own editing, animating, compositing, special effects, sound mixing and sound creation. You can even burn your movies to a DVD. There are numerous packages and stand-alone programs available.

For editing, two of the most popular programs are **Adobe Premiere** and **Apple's Final Cut Pro**. I have always used Adobe's software and have been very happy with it, but I have also heard great things about **Final Cut Pro**. To get more information on either product, check out their websites at **www.adobe.com** or **www.finalcutpro.com**. Once your movie is edited, you might need to do some animation, blue screen removal or compositing. One of the most popular products for this is **Adobe After Effects**. You might also need some painting work done, and Adobe offers an excellent program for this called **Photoshop**. You might think I'm starting to sound like an Adobe salesman, but I just think they have some excellent products. There are a lot of other programs available from other companies that offer outstanding quality and power, and would also fulfill all of your editing needs.

When you are buying your software, you can receive a huge discount if you or someone you know is a student or works for a school district. There are several companies that will give educational discounts, and several of them can be found with an Internet search. One of the companies that I use is **www.studentmarket.com**. I purchased the **Adobe Video Collection** for $399, while it retails for $999.

With the software that's available, you can learn how to do almost anything with your movies. The only limit is your imagination.

EDITING SOFTWARE

Editing software for a computer is called an NLE (non-linear editing) system. These programs allow you to take all of your different video clips, pictures, sounds, music and titles and combine them together to make your final movie. You can take your video clips and edit them, add effects, add voice-overs, mix soundtracks and arrange your elements to create your masterpiece. Here is a list of some of the more popular programs.

Adobe Premiere Pro
Adobe Systems, Inc.
www.adobe.com
(800) 833-6687

Final Cut Pro
Apple
www.apple.com
(800) 692-7753

Avid Xpress Pro
Avid Technology
www.avid.com
(800) 949-2843

Liquid Edition
Pinnacle Systems
www.pinnaclesys.com
(650) 526-1600

Vegas
Sony Electronics
www.sonystyle.com
(877) 865-7669

COMPOSITING SOFTWARE

Compositing software allows you to combine multiple images into one single image. It allows you to create motion graphics and visual effects. Some of the features provided by compositing software are animation tools for text and images, adding creative visual effects, adding and editing masks, color correction, rotoscoping, painting, and working with transparency, keying and mattes. These are the programs that are made to work with blue screens and image manipulation. Here is a list of some of the more popular programs.

Adobe After Effects
Adobe Systems, Inc.
www.adobe.com
(800) 833-6687

Motion
Apple
www.apple.com
(800) 692-7753

Avid FX
Avid Technology
www.avid.com
(800) 949-2843

PAINTING SOFTWARE

Painting software, also called image editing software, allows you to manipulate images or video frames in almost any way imaginable. You can paint over them, add text, add dozens of layers of images on top of each other, replace or match colors, correct red eye, add filters, add effects, work with masks and blue screens and change the characteristics of the images such as size, shape, brightness, transparency and contrast. This is just a sampling of the tools available. There are several programs that fall into this category, but the program you will probably want to use is **Adobe Photoshop**. This program is the industry standard.

Adobe Photoshop
Adobe Systems, Inc.
www.adobe.com
(800) 833-6687

Twister
VDS
www.videodesignsoftware.com
(631) 249-4399

Paint Shop Pro
Corel
www.corel.com
(800) 772-6735

TITLING SOFTWARE

Titling software can help you create stunning professional graphics and video titles. There are three different ways to get a good titling program. Most editing software programs, like **Adobe Premiere Pro** or **Final Cut Pro**, have a built-in tool for adding titles. These titling tools are already included as part of the program and they are normally very good. Other companies make titling plug-ins for the more popular editing programs. These plug-ins either add titling tools to your editing program, or they enhance the tools that are already included. The last option is buy a stand-alone program to create your titles, and then import them into your editing application.

Titlemotion
Inscriber
Plug-in for Adobe Premiere
Plug-in for Avid Xpress Pro
Plug-in for DPS Velocity
Plug-in for Media 100
www.inscriber.com
(800) 363-3400

Adobe Photoshop
Adobe Systems, Inc.
Stand-alone program
www.adobe.com
(800) 833-6687

Wild FX Pro Title Generator & Text Animator
Wildform
Stand-alone program
www.titlingsoftware.com
(310) 559-2025

3D SOFTWARE

3D software allows you to create almost anything you can imagine. Alien worlds, futuristic vehicles and amazing robots are all within your grasp. With a little training and a big imagination, there is no end to the creatures, places and effects you can create.

Lightwave 3D
Newtek
www.newtek.com
(800) 847-6111

3ds Max
Discreet
www.discreet.com
(800) 440-4198

Maya
Alias
www.alias.com
(866) 226-8859

SOUND SOFTWARE

Sound software allows you to edit your sounds or create new ones. You can add effects, change attributes, mix audio tracks, balance sound levels, and create custom fades. Sound software allows you to trim unwanted sections and synchronize audio with video.

Sound Forge
Sony
www.sonymediasoftware.com
(800) 577-6642

Adobe Audition
Adobe Systems, Inc.
www.adobe.com
(800) 833-6687

Logic Pro
Apple
www.apple.com
(408) 996-1010

Pro Tools
Avid Technology
www.avid.com
(800) 949-2843

MUSIC CREATION SOFTWARE

Music enhances the emotion and mood of any movie. What would *Star Wars* or *Titanic* be without the emotional adrenaline rush created by the musical score? Music flows to the core of our body, attaching us to the characters and story in a way that nothing else can. In other words, music is extremely important. After you film and edit your movie masterpiece, how do you get the right music to finish the project? If you are not a musician yourself, you still have several options available to you. You can pay someone else to create the score, you can lease the music from companies that create scores, you can buy royalty-free music libraries and choose which music you want, or you can create it yourself with music creation software. Here are some of the more popular music creation software programs.

Sonic Fire Pro
SmartSound
www.smartsound.com
(800) 454-1900

Acid Music Studio
Sony
www.sonystyle.com
(877) 865-7669

Music Creator Pro
Cakewalk
www.cakewalk.com
(888) 225-3925

Band in a Box
PG Music
www.pgmusic.com
(800) 268-6272

MUSIC LIBRARIES

When creating the musical score for your movie, you can purchase royalty-free music or lease already-created scores in a multitude of genres. Here are a few companies that offer these types of services.

BackTraxx
Digital Juice, Inc.
www.digitaljuice.com
(800) 525-2203

Megatrax Production Music
Megatrax
www.megatrax.com
(888) 634-2555

Music 2 Hues Production Music Library
Music 2 Hues
www.music2hues.com
(888) 821-7515

The Music Bakery Royalty-Free Music
The Music Bakery
www.musicbakery.com
(800) 229-0313

SOFTWARE PACKAGES

There are some great software packages available that include several of the programs that you might need. Here are some of the more popular packages.

Adobe Video Collection
Adobe Premiere Pro
Adobe After Effects
Adobe Audition
Adobe Encore
Adobe Systems, Inc.
www.adobe.com
(800) 833-6687

Final Cut Studio
Final Cut Pro
Motion 2
Soundtrack Pro
DVD Studio Pro
Apple
www.apple.com
(800) 692-7753

Avid Xpress Studio
Avid Xpress Pro
Avid Pro Tools LE
Avid 3D
Avid FX
Avid DVD by Sonic
Avid Technology
www.avid.com
(800) 949-2843

ACADEMIC DISCOUNTS

If you or someone you know is a student or works for a school district, you can receive huge discounts on some of your software purchases. Here are some companies that offer these discounts.

StudentMarket
www.studentmarket.com
(888) 788-3348

Academic Superstore
www.academicsuperstore.com
(800) 817-2347

Gradware
www.gradware.com
(800) 472-3583

JourneyEd
www.journeyed.com
(800) 874-9001

StudentDiscounts
www.studentdiscounts.com
(877) 762-7876

Advanced Academic Solutions
www.advancedacademic.com
(866) 923-9473

SECTION 12

BLUE/GREEN SCREENS

What is a Blue Screen and what is it used for? A Blue Screen allows you to film someone or something and then replace the background with whatever you want. You can show someone flying up in the clouds, or walking on the moon, or entering a futuristic city, or anything else your imagination can come up with. Here is how it works. First, you need a Blue Screen. Actually, this can be any color you want, but blue and green are the most common. Whatever color you choose, the same color cannot be in your actor's clothes, props or anything else. The Blue Screen is like a giant backdrop. Imagine a giant blue or green curtain behind your actors. The color has to be exactly the same on the entire screen, and you will want to use lights to brighten the screen. You must be careful to light the screen evenly, because you do not want hot spots that are brighter than other parts of the screen. In your camera shot, you only want to see your actors and their props — everything else should be blue or green.

A Blue Screen can be made from many different things. A good site to get some ideas is **www.studiodepot.com**; and check out their Special Effects section. You can use blue or green paint, or special paint called **Chroma Key Blue** or **Chroma Key Green**. By using paint, you can cover a multitude of 2D and 3D surfaces with the exact same color. They also offer **Chroma Key** spray paint. You can also use blue or green fabric or cloth, which is inexpensive and easy to work with and store. Another option is bright blue or green poster board. Poster board can usually be found for under $1 a sheet. Another alternative is **Chroma Paper**, which can come in all different sizes. You can also use **Chroma Tape**, which can be used to secure other screens, or to hide cords and similar items. There are always other options, but this gives you a good idea of what is available.

In addition to the Blue Screen, you will need a computer program that allows you to work with Blue Screens. Both **Adobe Premiere** and **Adobe After Effects** will allow you to use Blue Screens, although After Effects will give you a lot more options and more control than Adobe Premiere.

Basically, the software will remove the Blue Screen background and replace it with whatever you want. You can make the new background a video shot from a different location, shots of some miniatures, a futuristic city that you created with a 3D program, or anything else your imagination can come up with. Some of the most famous movies of all time used Blue Screens to create some of their most spectacular effects: *Star Wars*, *E.T.*, *Lord of the Rings*, the *Terminator* series and many more. This effect gives you access to shots that would otherwise be impossible.

The following tutorial was done on **Adobe Premiere Pro 1.5**, but the concepts will work with many other versions and software programs.

* *This section includes information from Likeastory.com.*

This picture shows a miniature house with a Blue Screen behind it.

This picture shows the background that will replace the Blue Screen.

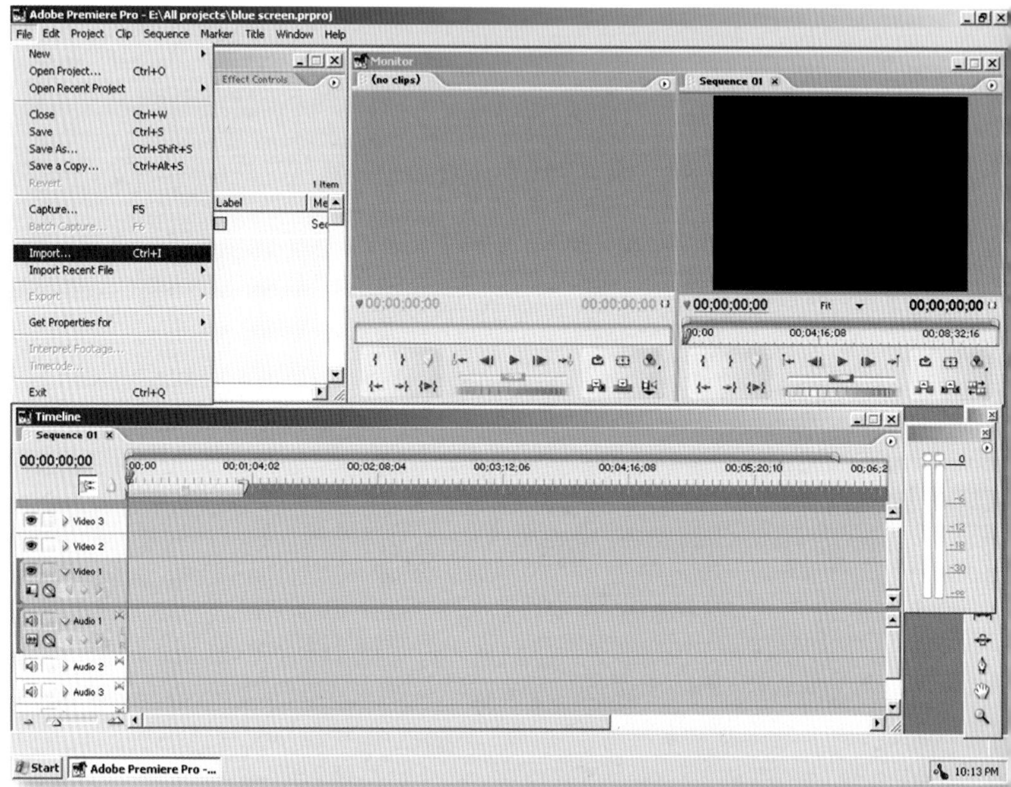

After you open **Adobe Premiere Pro 1.5**, click on **File, Import**.

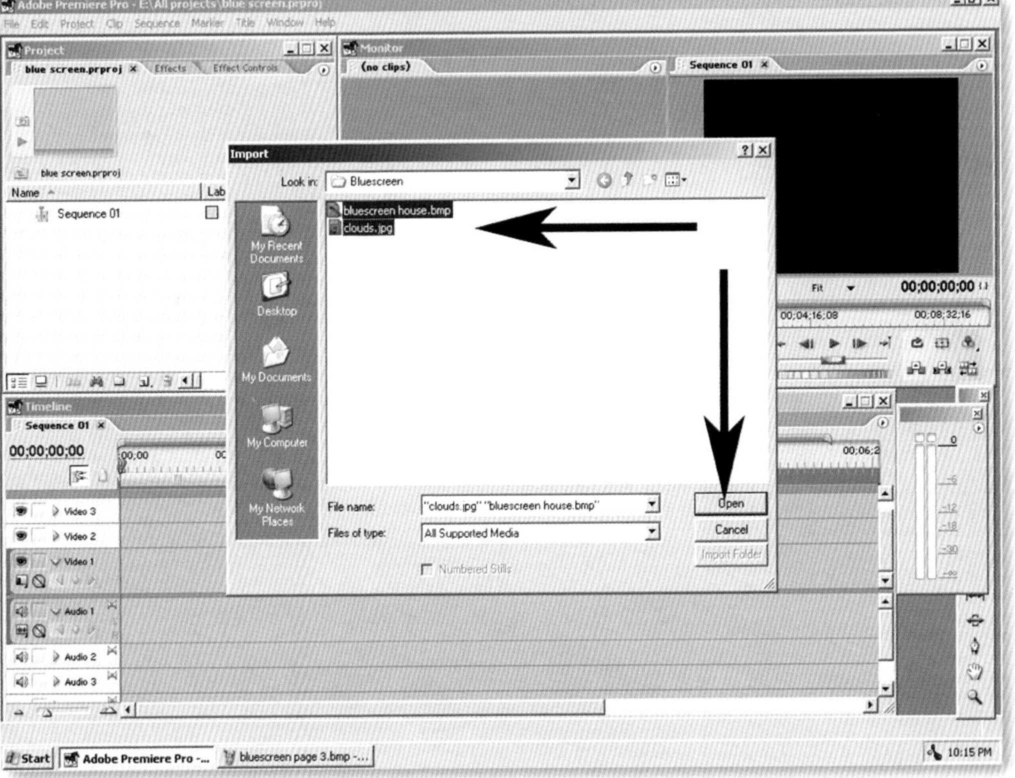

Highlight the files you want and click **Open**. The files in the above example are named **bluescreen house.bmp** and **clouds.jpg**.

Your files will be listed in the **Project** window.

Click on the video clip that will be replacing the Blue Screen and drag it down to **Video 1** in the **Timeline**. In the above example, the video clip is **clouds.jpg**.

Click on **Project**, **Project Settings**, **General**.

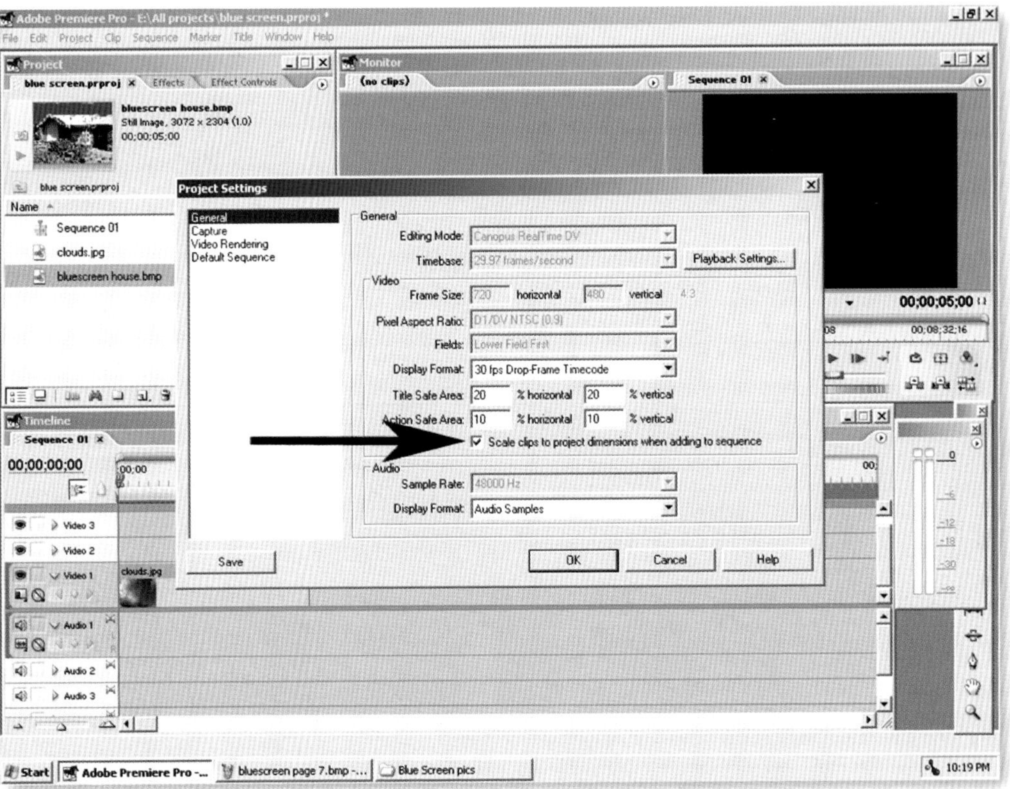

Place a checkmark in the box next to **Scale clips to project dimensions when adding to sequence**. Click **OK**.

Drag the clip with the Blue Screen in it down to **Video 2** in the **Timeline**. In the example above, the clip is called **bluescreen house.bmp**.

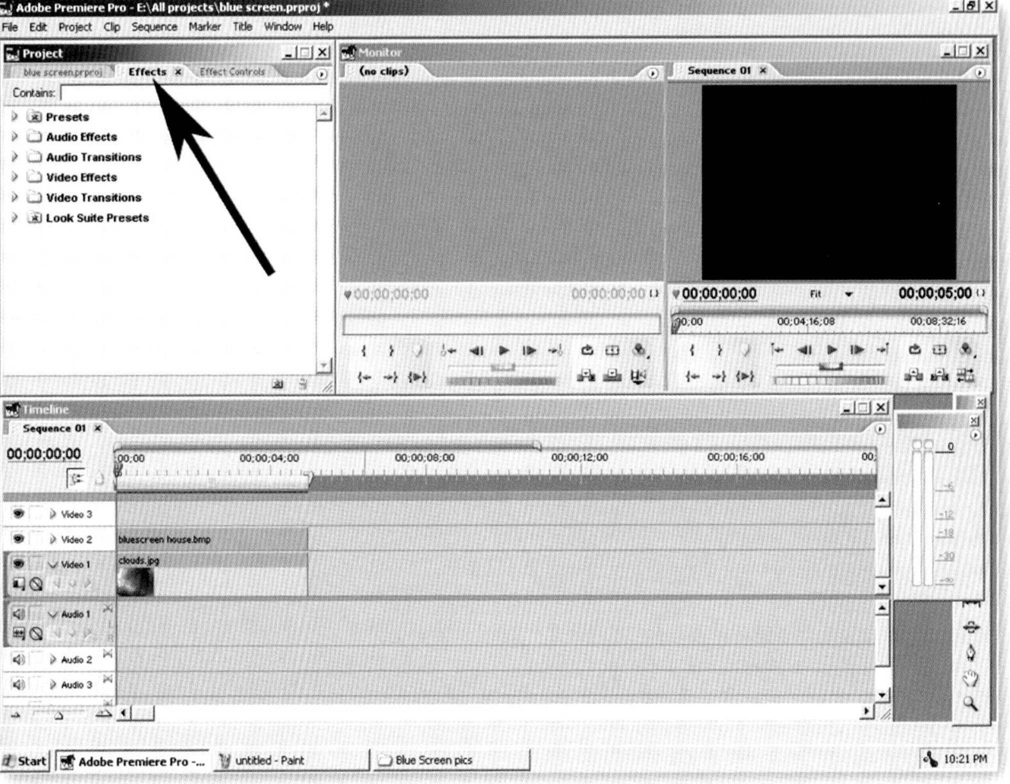

Click on the **Effects** tab.

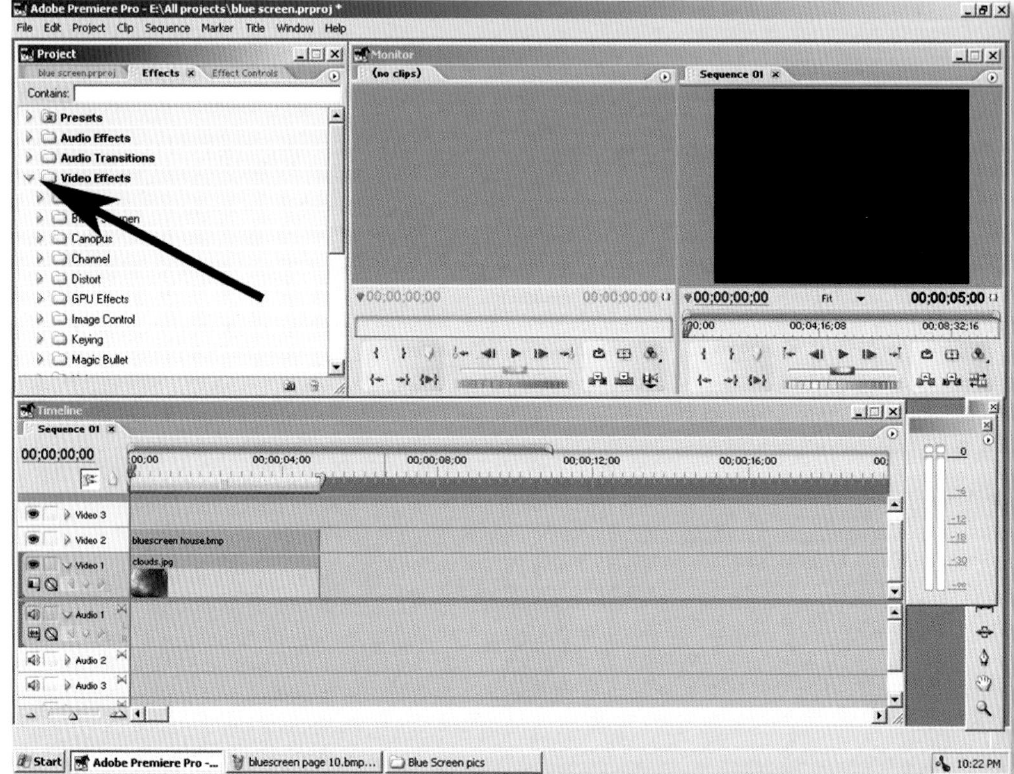

Click on the small triangle next to **Video Effects**.

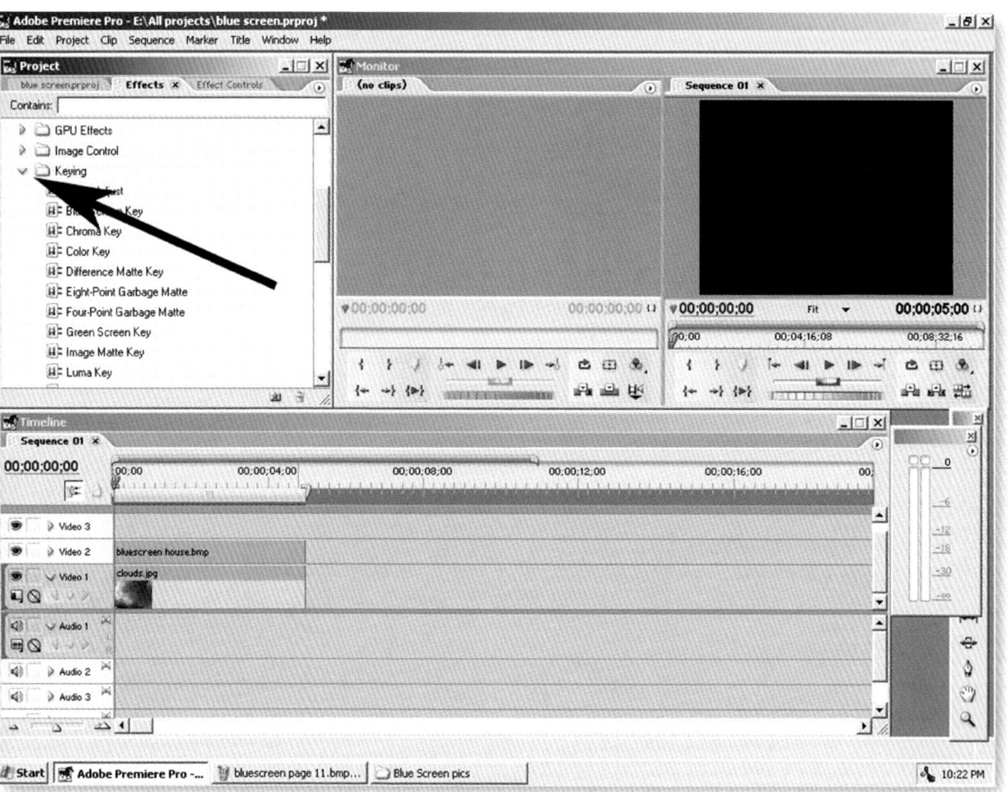

Click on the small triangle next to **Keying**.

Click on **Blue Screen Key** and drag it onto the clip in **Video 2** in the **Timeline**.

Press **Enter** on the keyboard to render the video clips. The line above the clips will turn green once the rendering is done.

Click on **File**, **Save**.

This picture shows the final shot.

This picture shows the house with a night sky.

This picture shows the house on a rainy night.

This picture shows the house with smoke behind it.

SECTION 13

TELEPORTER EFFECT

In the Physical Effects section of this book, we showed you how to make someone disappear. The Teleporter effect is very similar, except that the person slowly fades away instead of suddenly disappearing. Again, you need to film two shots, one with your actor in the scene and one without your actor in the scene. Be sure to use a tripod so that both shots are exactly the same and that the camera does not move at all. The following tutorial was done with **Adobe Premiere Pro 1.5**, but the concepts will work with many other versions and software programs.

* *This section includes information from Likeastory.com*

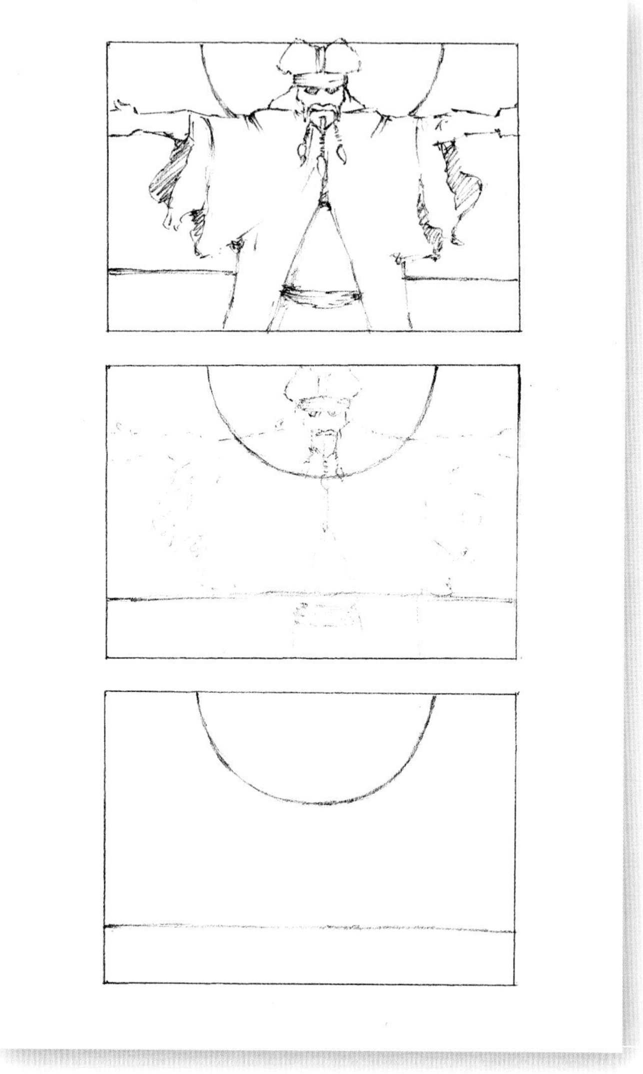

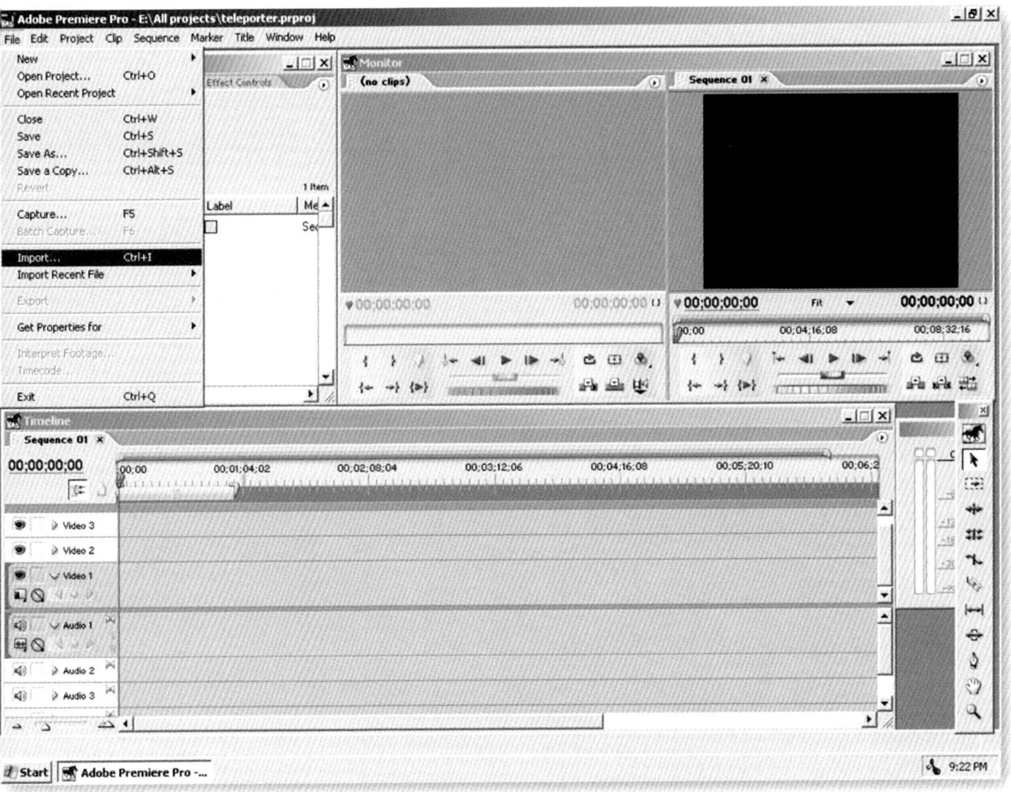

After you open **Adobe Premiere Pro 1.5**, click on **File**, **Import**.

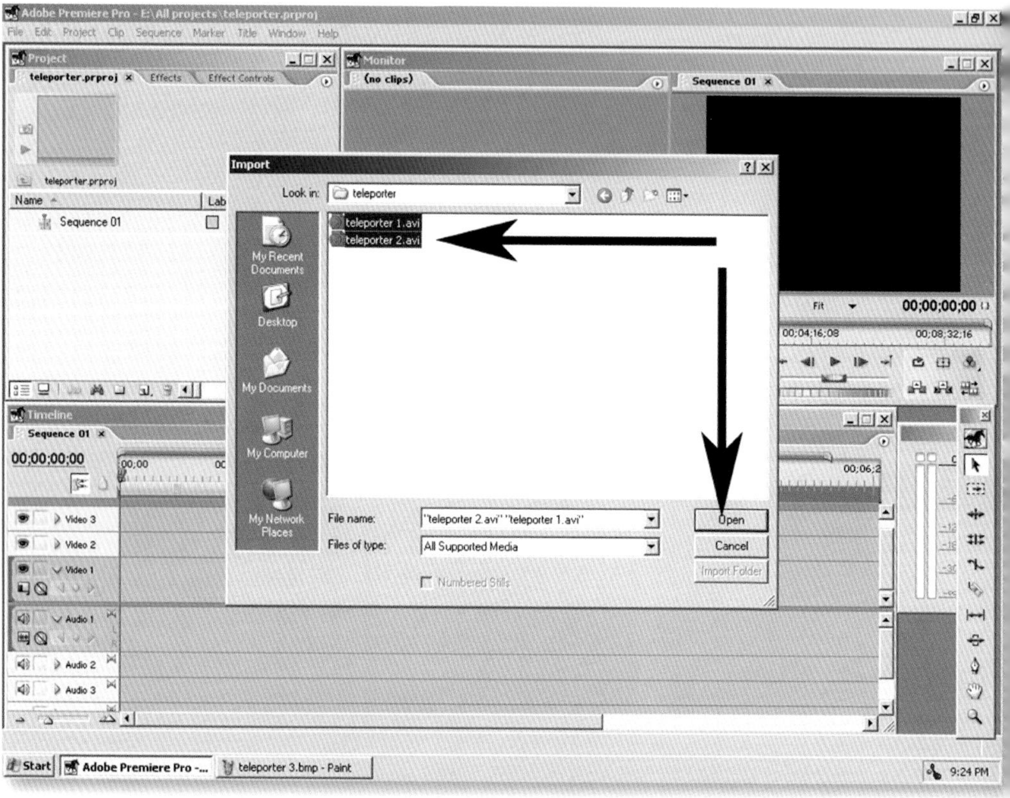

Highlight the two video clips and click **Open**. In the example above, the clips are named **teleporter 1.avi** and **teleporter 2.avi**.

This picture shows the two clips imported into **Premiere**.

Click and drag the clip with the actor in it to the **Video 2 timeline**. In the example above, the clip is named **teleporter 1.avi**.

Click and drag the clip without the actor in it to the **Video 1 timeline**. In the example above, the clip is named **teleporter 2.avi**. Place it slightly to the right of the other clip as in the example above.

Click on the **Effects** tab.

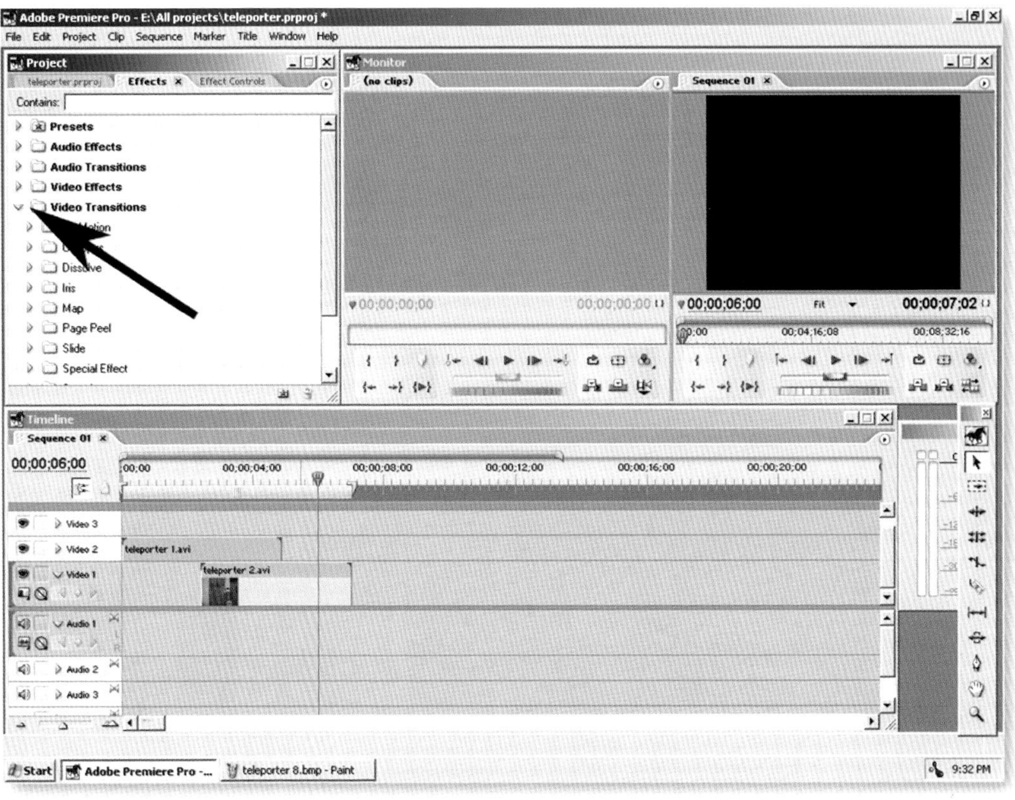

Click on the small triangle next to **Video Transitions**.

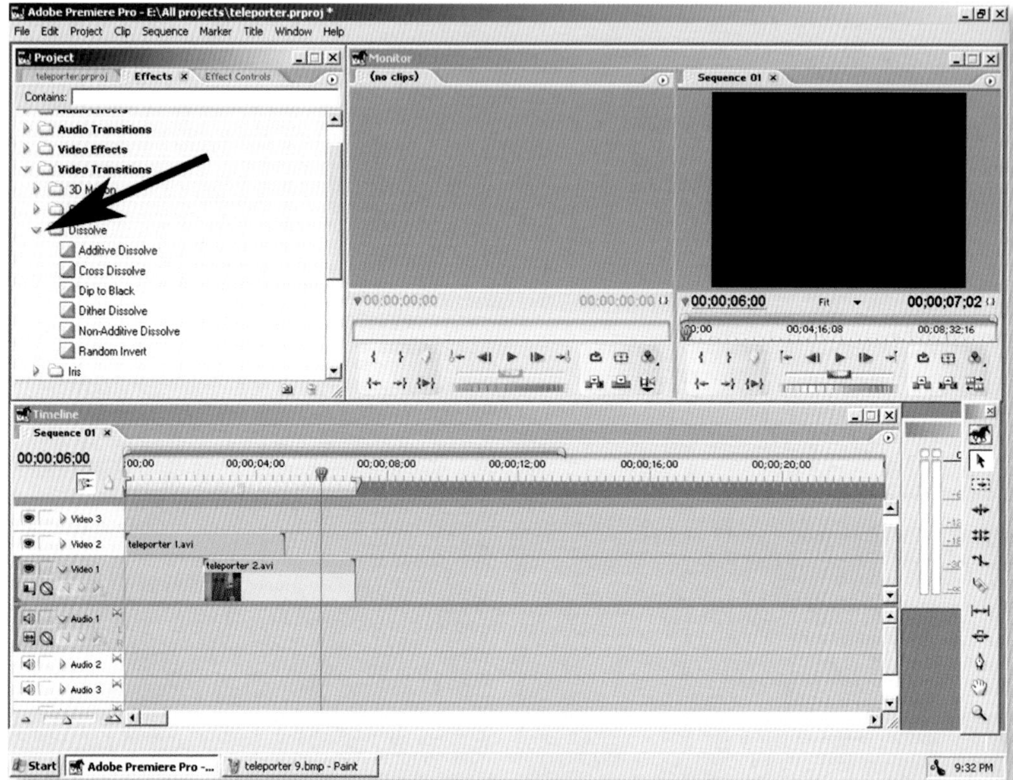

Click on the small triangle next to **Dissolve**.

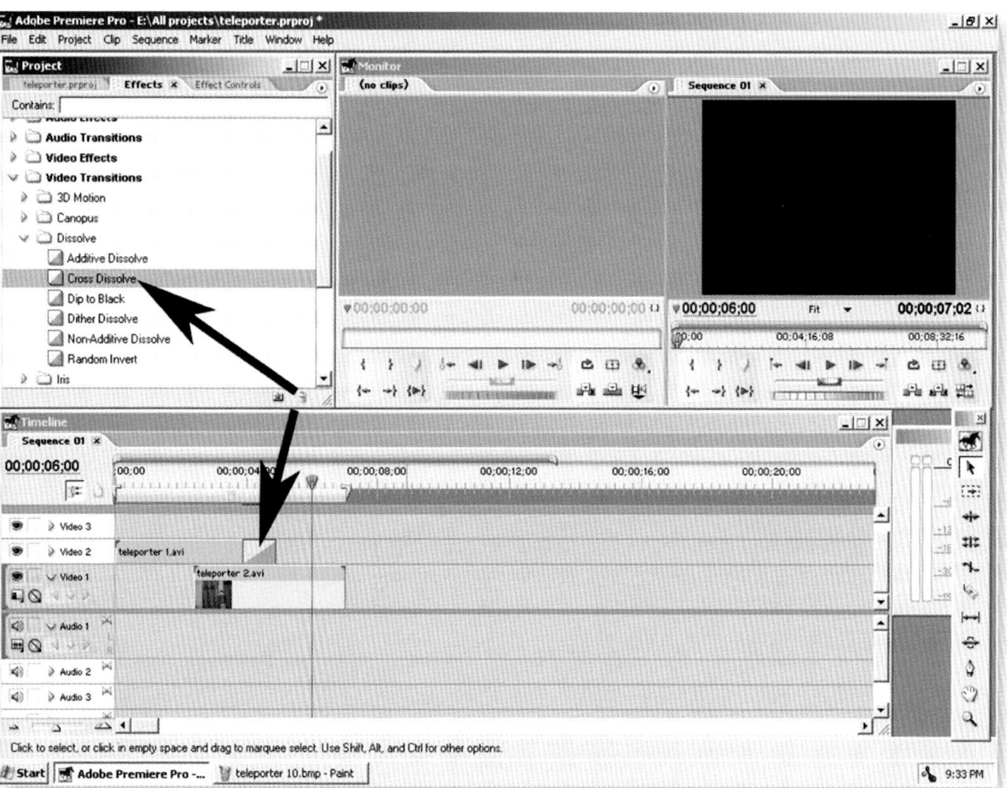

Click and drag the **Cross Dissolve** effect to the end of the clip in the **Video 2 timeline**.

Expand the **Cross Dissolve** effect to cover the area where the two clips overlap each other.

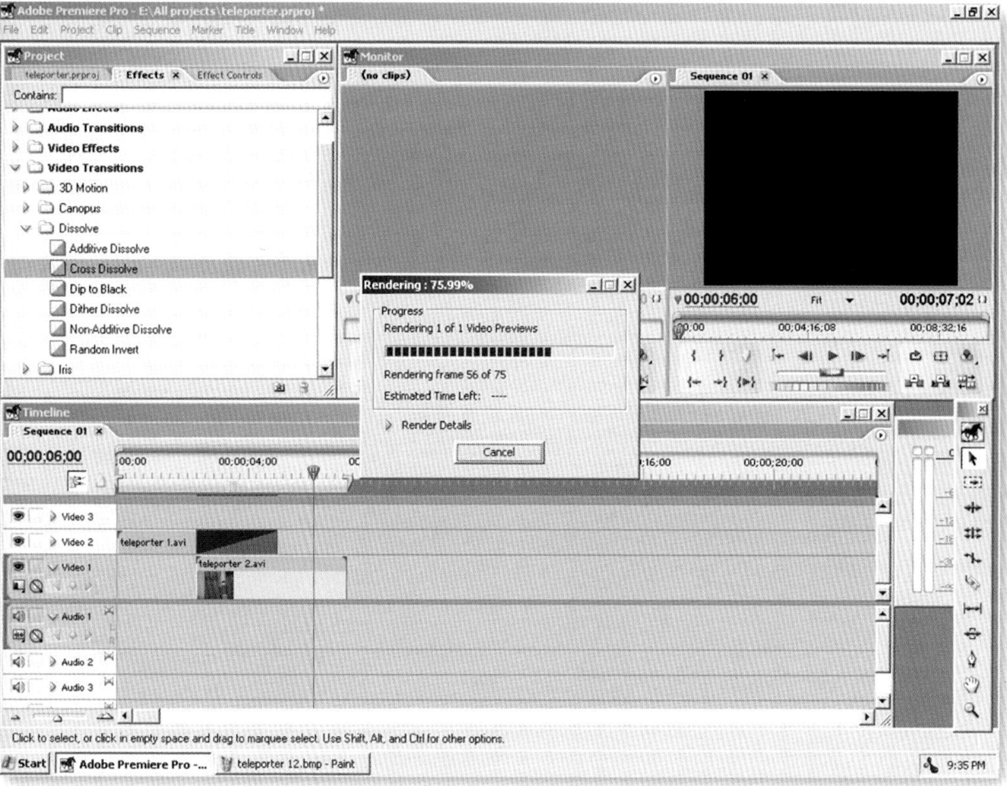

Press the **Enter** key to render the clips.

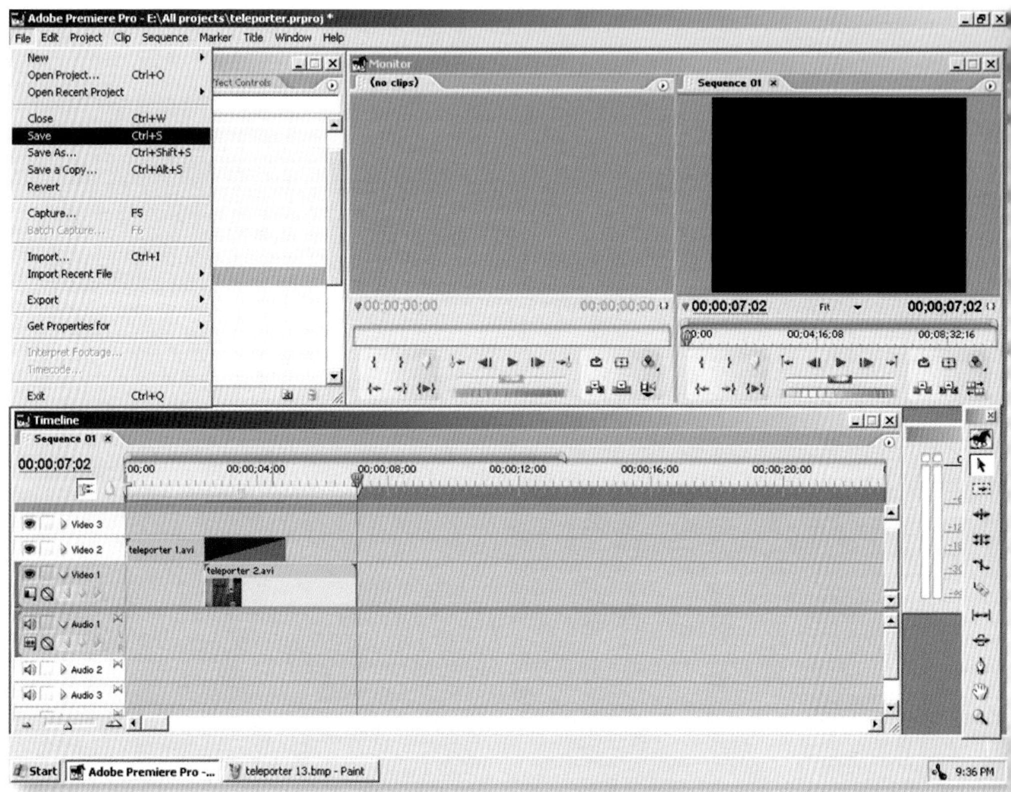

Click on **File**, **Save**.

SECTION 14

GUN FLASHES

There is no mistaking the unique flash of light that exits the gun barrel as each bullet is fired out. But unless you have a lot of money and a pyrotechnics license, this is a difficult effect to create. Here are a few options for the beginner and independent filmmaker. The first option is to use the software **FXhome**. This software is showcased in the back of this book. This is an amazing program that is very inexpensive. One of its many features is that it allows you to quickly and easily add gun flashes to your movie. It comes with several different gun flash styles that you can manipulate and change to your needs. It has front flashes and side flashes, and can really help create bang for your buck.

Another way to create the Gun Flash effect is with a paint program like **Adobe Photoshop**. The following tutorial was done with **Adobe Photoshop 7** and **Adobe Premiere Pro 1.5**, but the concepts will work with many other versions and software programs.

As with many effects, half of the illusion is the sound. A good gunshot sound is needed to complete the effect. Please see the section in this book called **A Word about Sound Effects**. With the Gun Flash effect, you will definitely want to "hear" the gunshot, as well as "see" it.

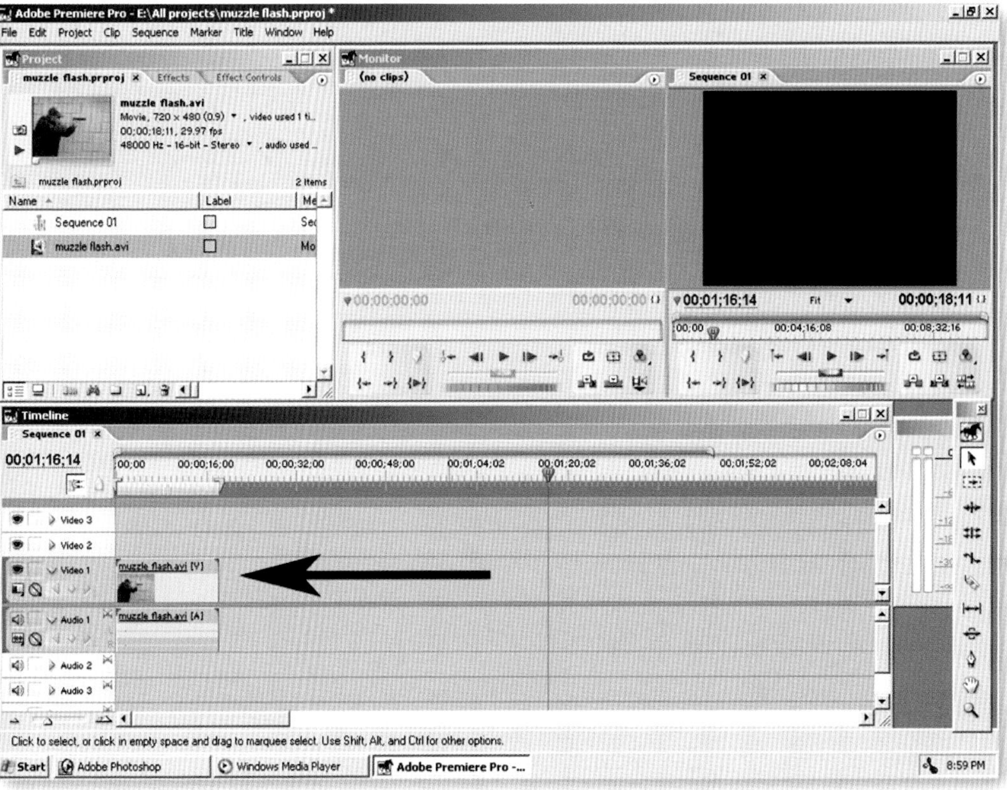

This picture shows your video clip in the timeline of **Adobe Premiere Pro**.

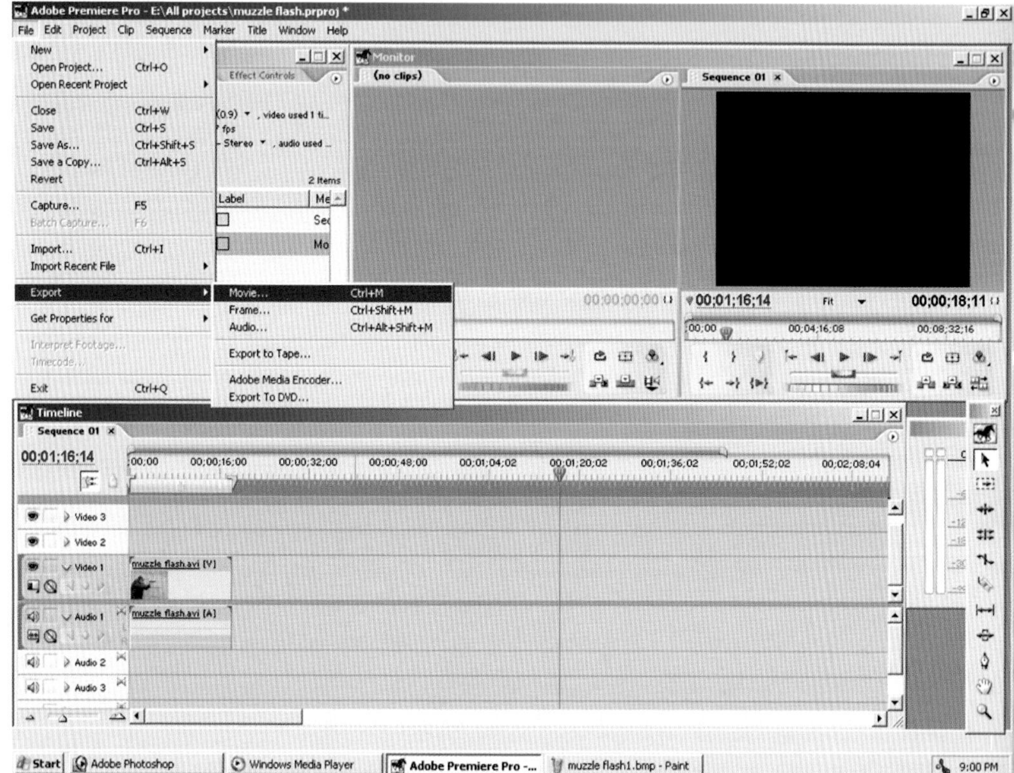

Click on **File**, **Export**, **Movie**.

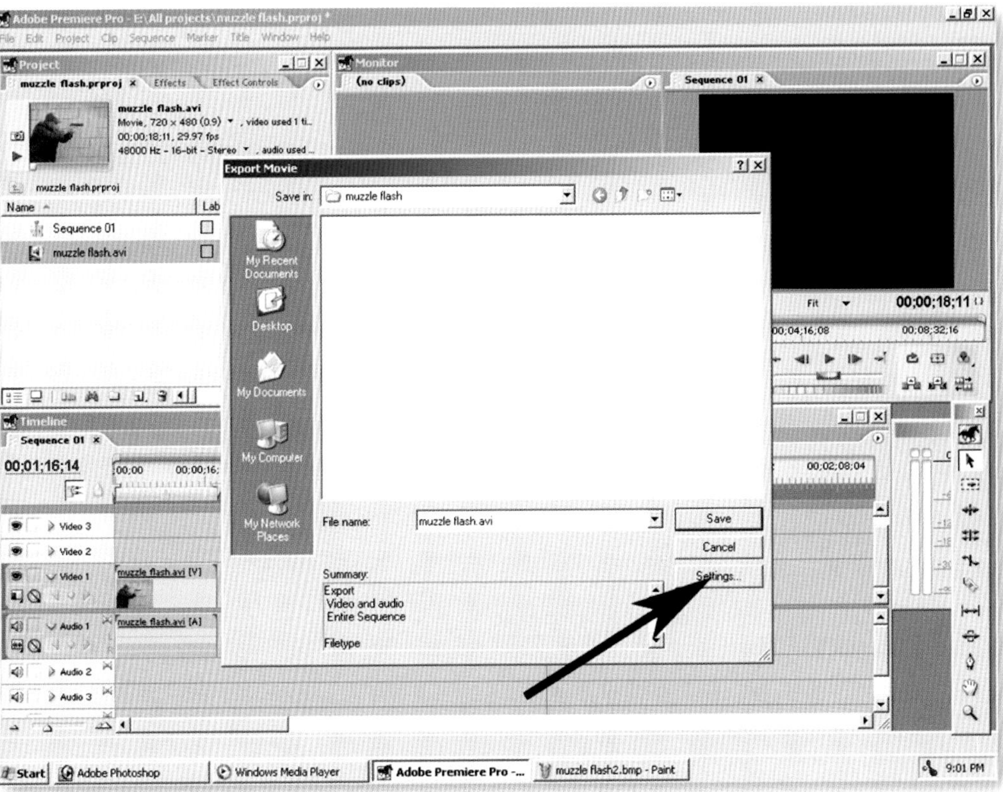

Click on **Settings**.

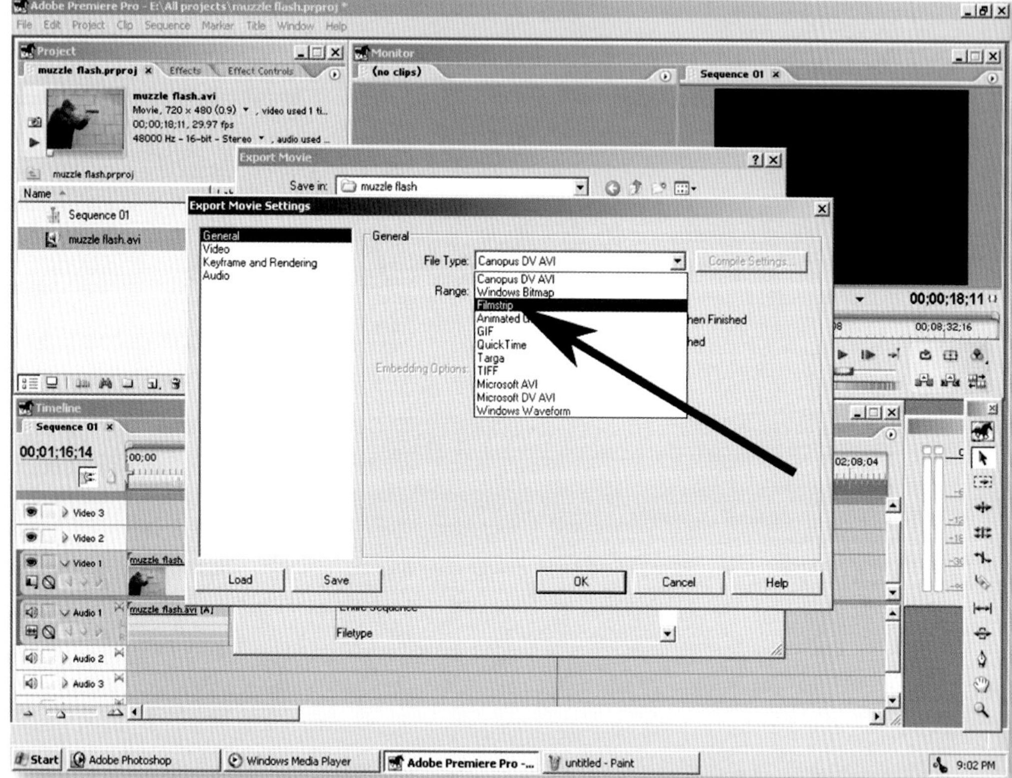

From the drop-down menu, click on **Filmstrip**.

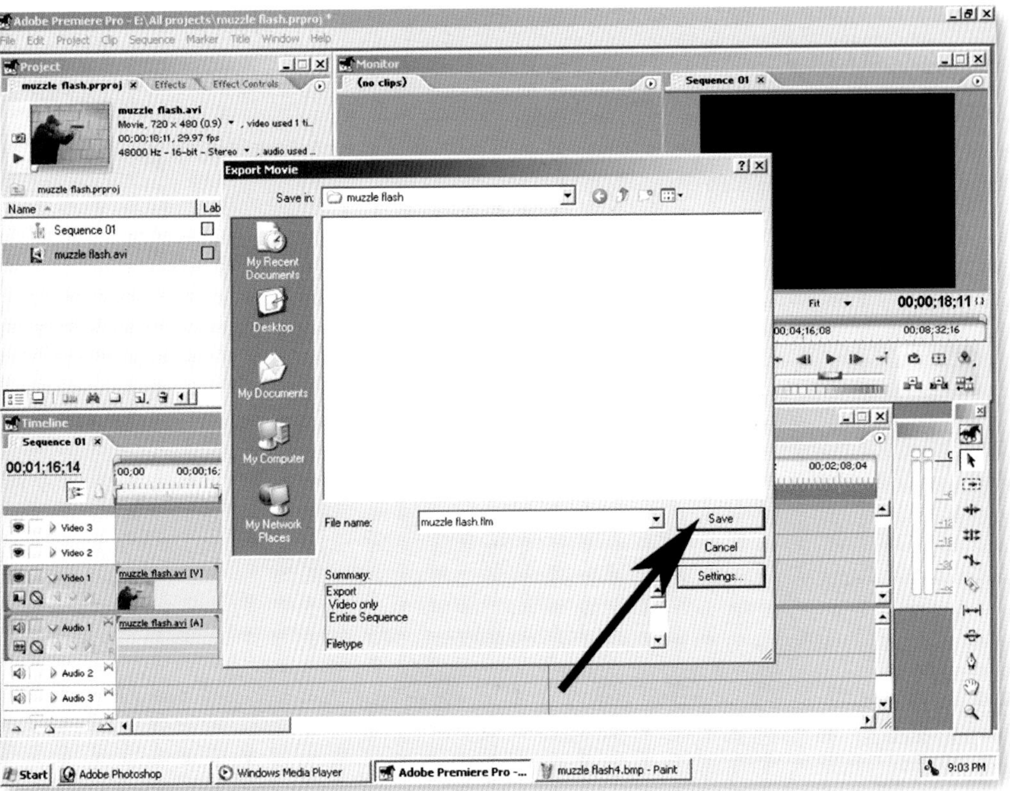

In the **File name:** field, type the name of your file. In the example above, we used the name **muzzle flash.flm**. Click on **Save**.

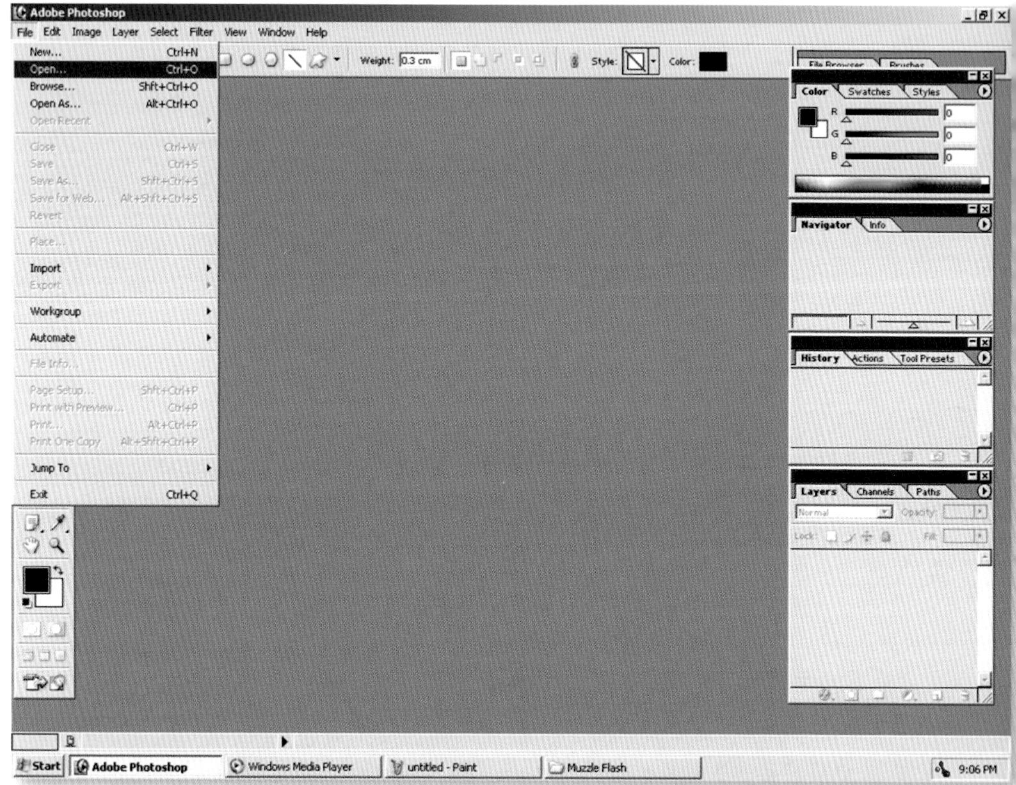

Start the program **Adobe Photoshop**. Click on **File**, **Open**.

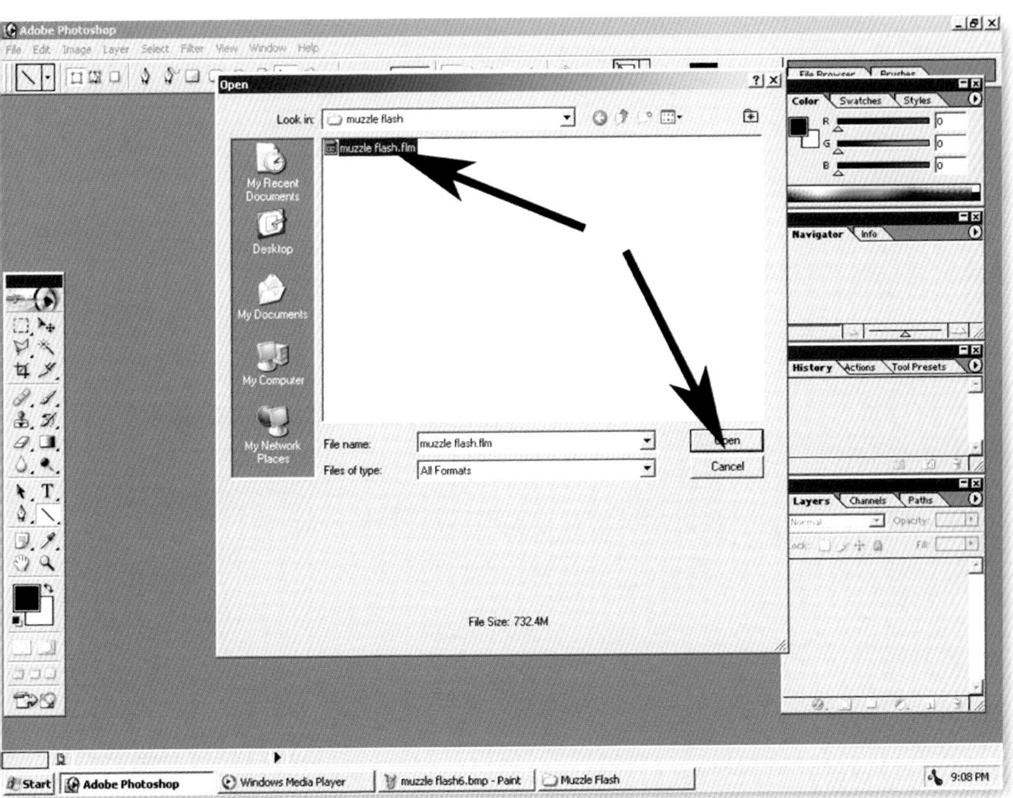

Highlight your file. In the above example, the file is called **muzzle flash.flm**. Click on **Open**.

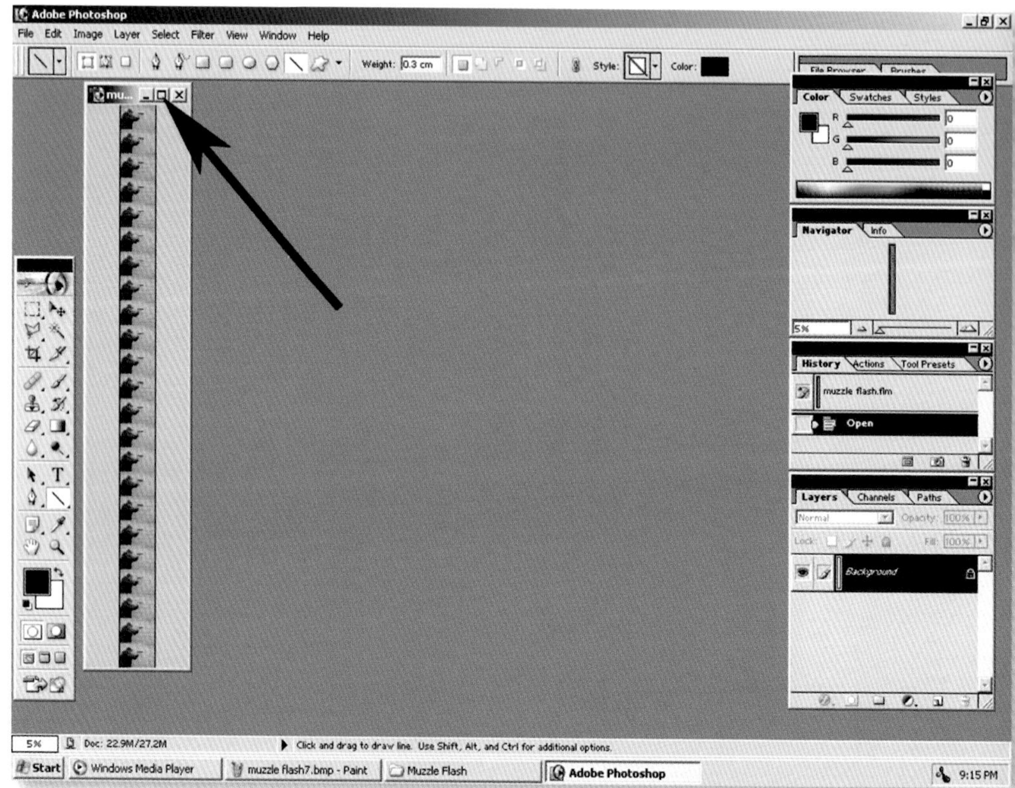

Click on the **Maximize** button.

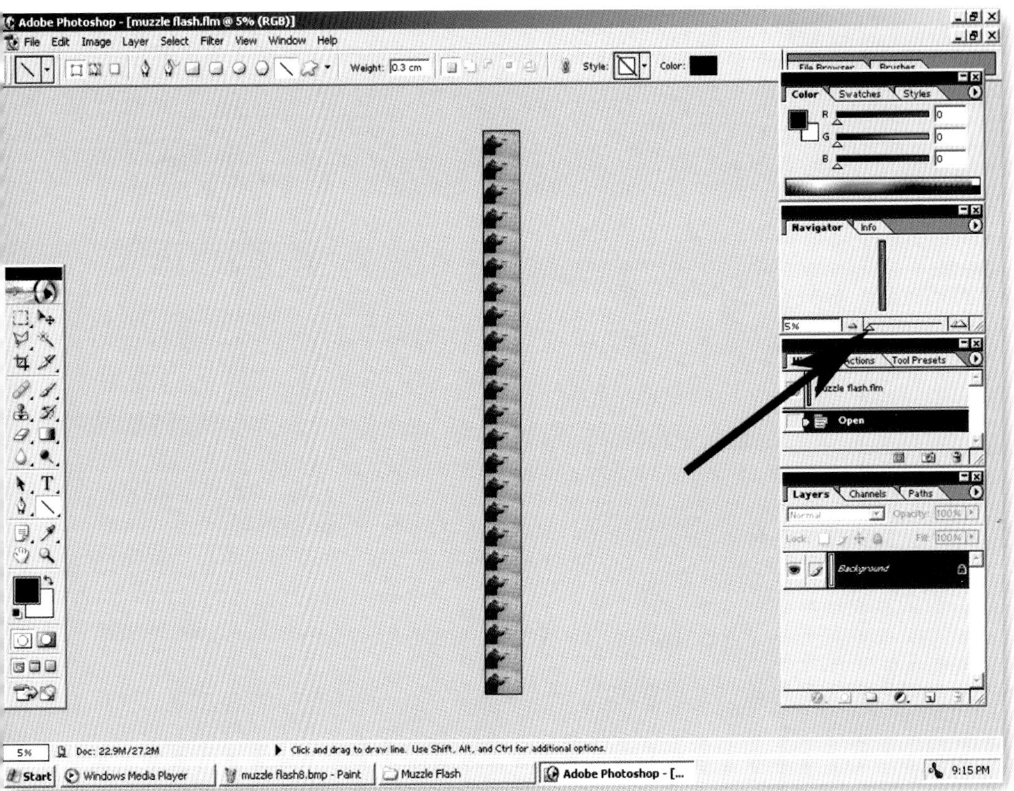

Click and drag the small triangle to the right. This will zoom in on your video clip.

Zoom in until you can easily see the frames of your video clip.

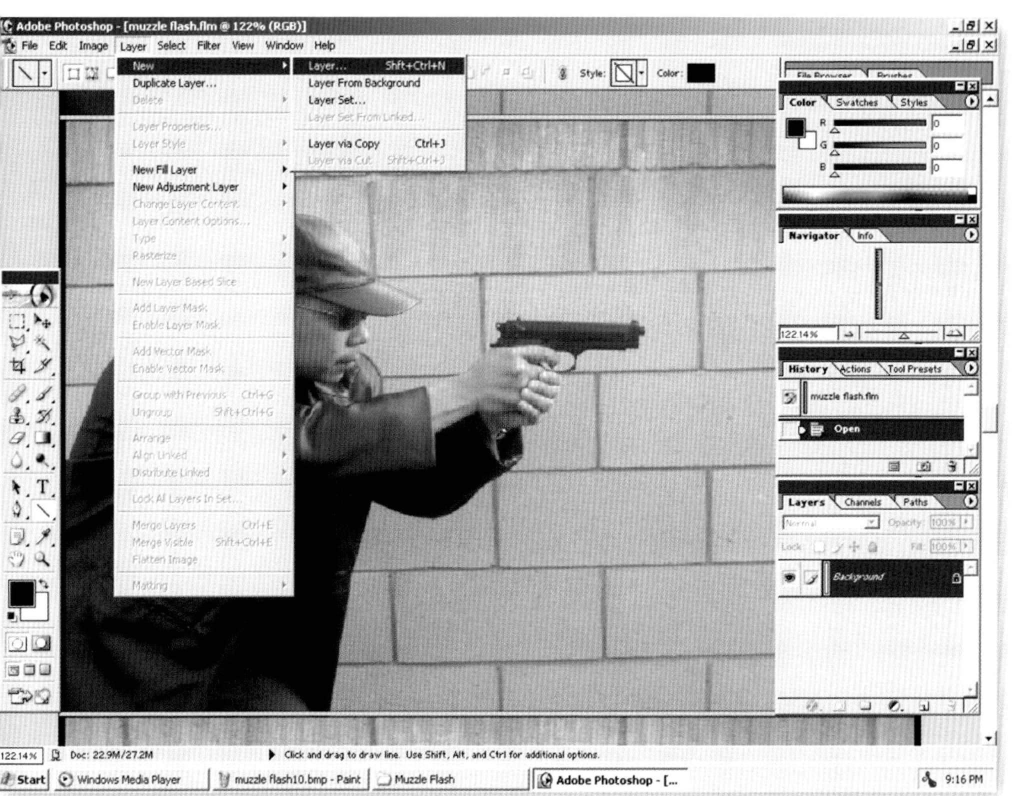

Click on **Layer**, **New**, **Layer**.

In the **Name:** field, type **Layer 2**. Click **OK**.

This box shows you what layers you have.

Click on the **Color Picker**.

Change the numbers in the **R:**, **G:** and **B:** fields to 255. Click **OK**. This will change the color to white.

Click on the **Paint Brush** tool.

Click on the **Brush Size** drop-down menu.

Click on **13** in the **Brush Size** menu.

Click and drag the small triangle to the right. This will zoom in on your video clip.

Using the **Paint Brush** tool, paint the gun flash protruding from the gun barrel. If you make a mistake, you can erase it with the **Eraser** tool. Watch an action movie DVD and pause the movie on the gun flashes. Use this picture as your reference to create your own flashes.

Click on the **Color Picker**.

Change the numbers in the **R:**, **G:** and **B:** fields. Change **R:** to 175, **G:** to 175 and **B:** to 30. Click **OK**. This will change the color to a shade of yellow.

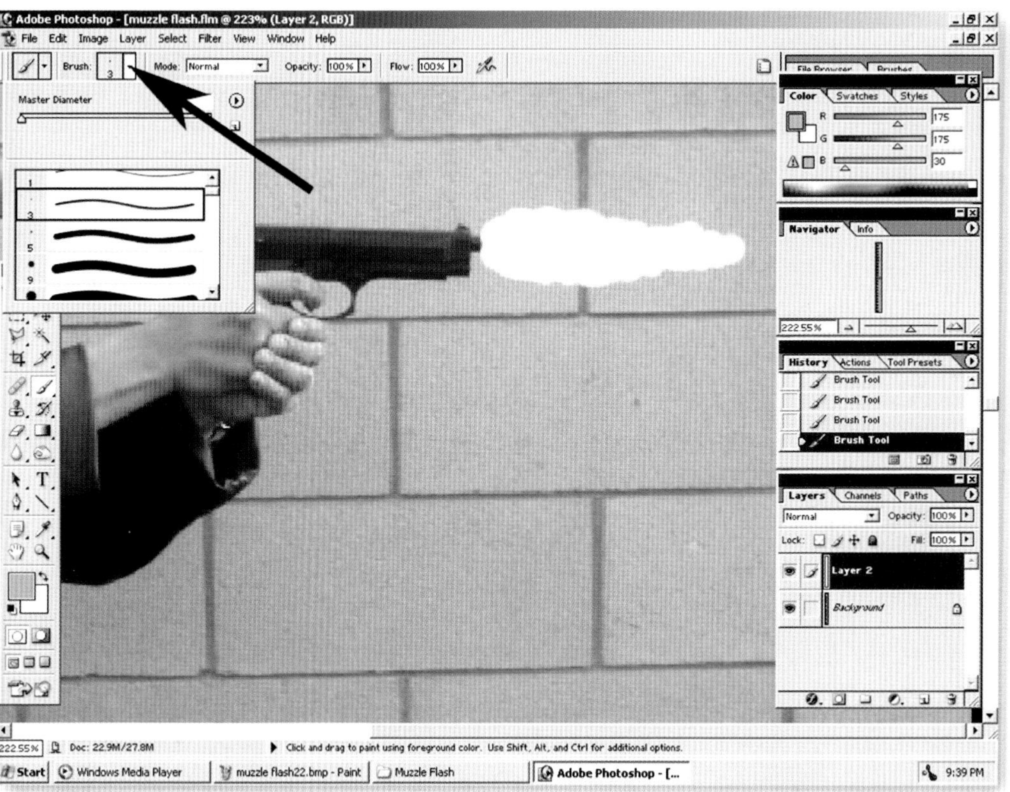

Change the **Brush Size** to **3**.

Paint small yellow dots around the edge of the gun flash.

Click the **Blur** tool.

Using the **Blur** tool, blur the yellow dots on the top of the gun flash.

Blur the remaining yellow dots.

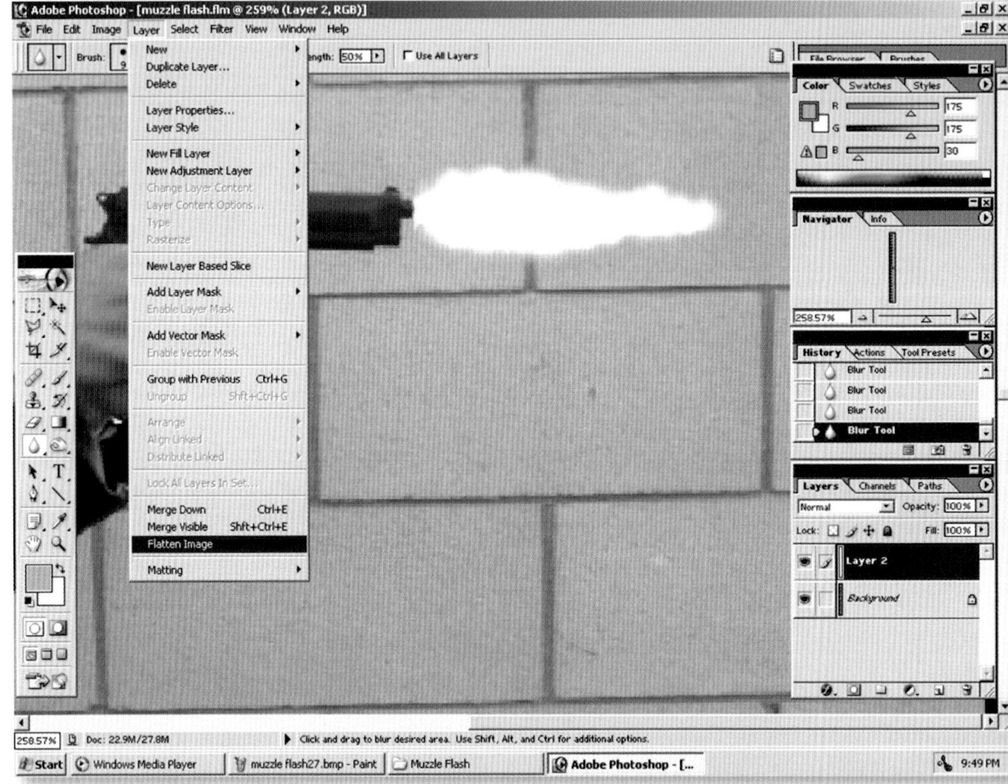

Click on **Layer**, **Flatten Image**.

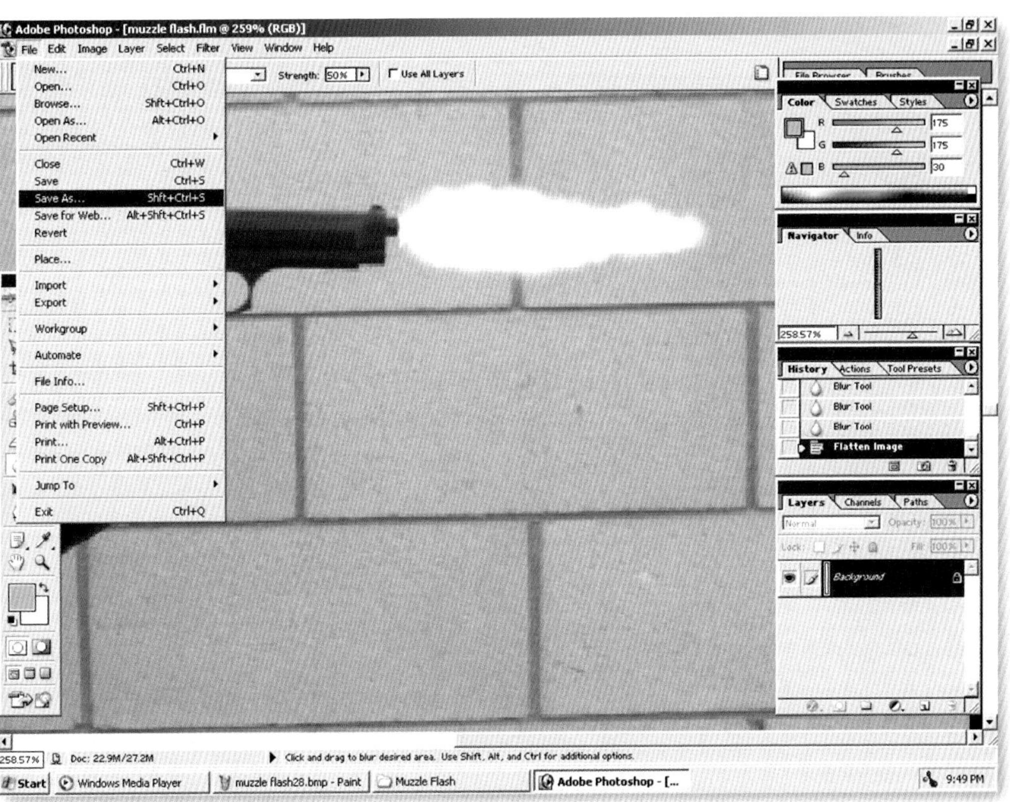

Click on **File**, **Save As**.

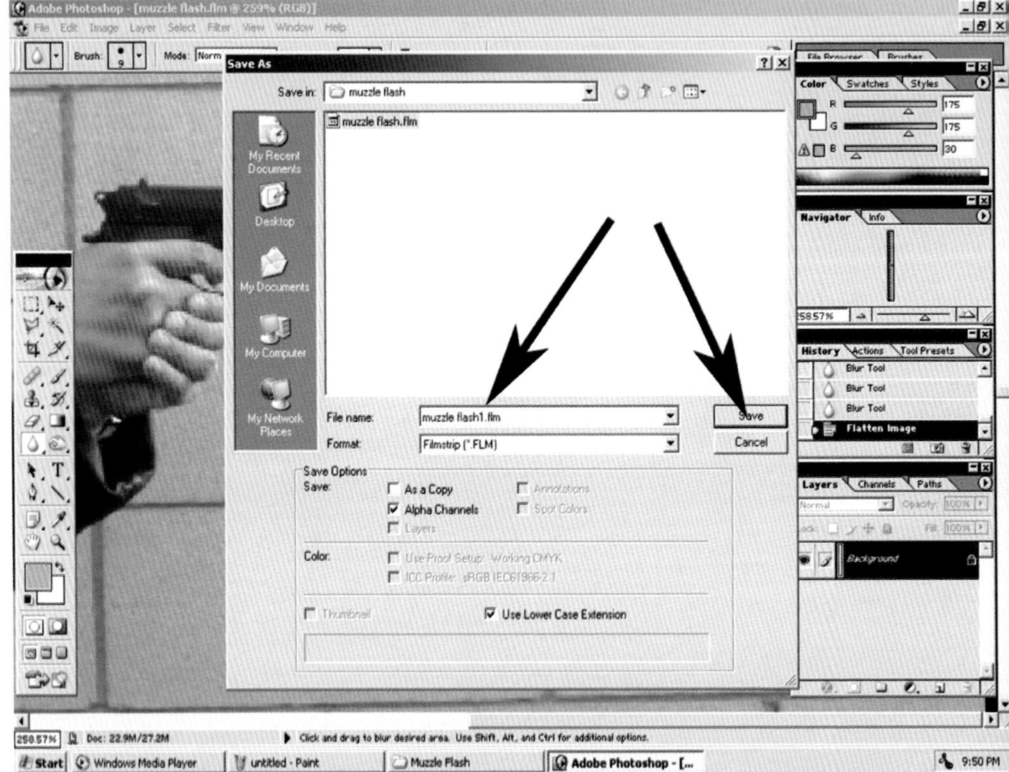

Check the **File Name:** and **Format:** fields and make sure they are correct. In the above example, we are saving the file as **muzzle flash1.flm**. We added the number **1** to the name so we know this video clip has been edited. You do not have to do this; you can leave the file name as **muzzle flash.flm**. Click **Save**. You can now open **Adobe Premiere Pro** and import your edited video clip.

SECTION 15

LIGHT SWORDS

What young boy has seen *Star Wars* and not dreamed of wielding a **lightsaber**? Until technology can catch up with our imaginations, we will have to rely on Special Effects. We are going to show you two ways to create this effect.

The first thing you will need is a Light Sword. The Light Sword effects will work if you only have a sword hilt, but they will work best if you have some sort of guide for where the blade will be. A good option that works well, and is fairly inexpensive, is to buy a toy **lightsaber** that has a telescoping blade. You now have a sword hilt for shots when the Light Sword is turned off, and you can easily extend the blade once the Light Sword is turned on. The long plastic blade will give you a guide when you are adding the effects. You can also put a wooden dowel or something similar in the sword hilt. This will also help if you have two people with Light Swords fighting each other. Having a blade will help to make the movements more believable.

The first way involves a computer program called **VisionLab** by **FXhome**. This is an inexpensive program and is also very easy to use. There is a section at the end of this book dedicated to this program and the company that created it. You can easily add Light Sword effects to your movies. You can change the color and the "look" of the swords, add special clashes when two Light Swords hit each other and almost anything else you can think of to create an exciting Light Sword battle. This program offers a lot of other Special Effects as well.

The second way to create the Light Sword effect is with a paint program like **Adobe Photoshop**. The following tutorial was done with **Adobe**

Photoshop 7 and **Adobe Premiere Pro 1.5**, but the concepts will work with many other versions and software programs.

As with many effects, half of the illusion is the sound. A good sound effect is needed to complete the Light Sword. Please see the section in this book called **A Word about Sound Effects**. With the Light Sword effect, you will definitely want to "hear" the Light Sword as well as "see" it.

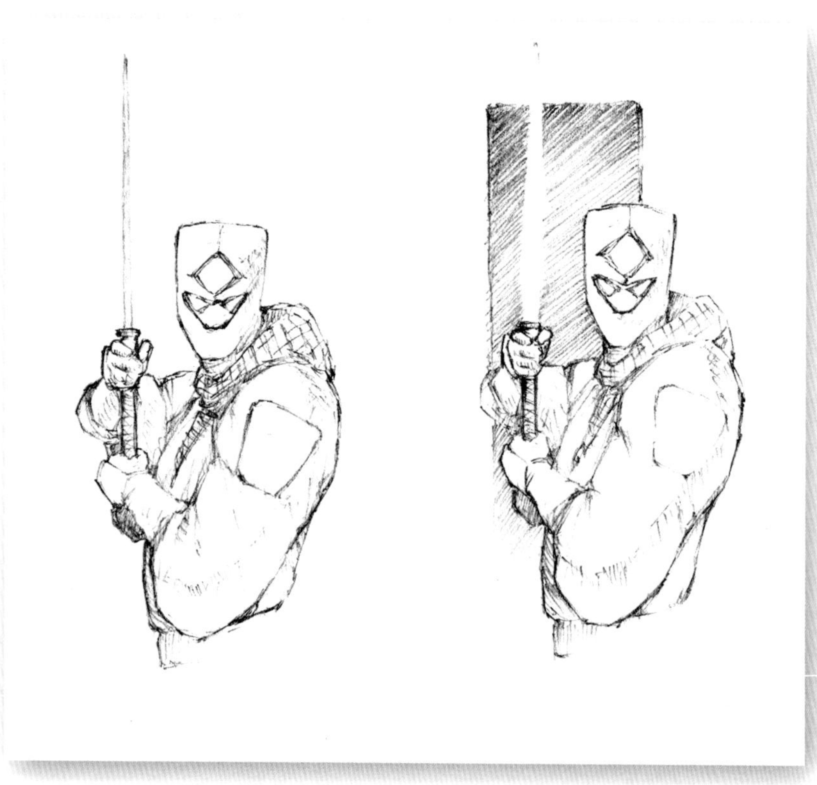

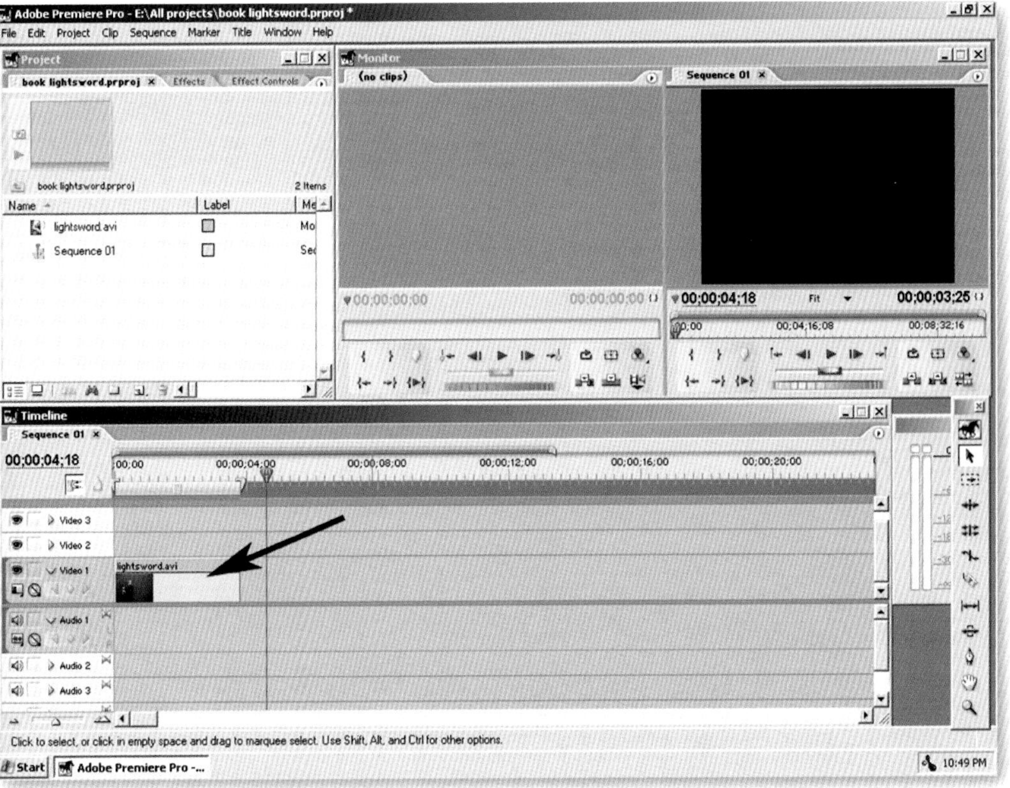

This picture shows your video clip in the timeline of **Adobe Premiere Pro**. In the above example, the clip is named **lightsword.avi**.

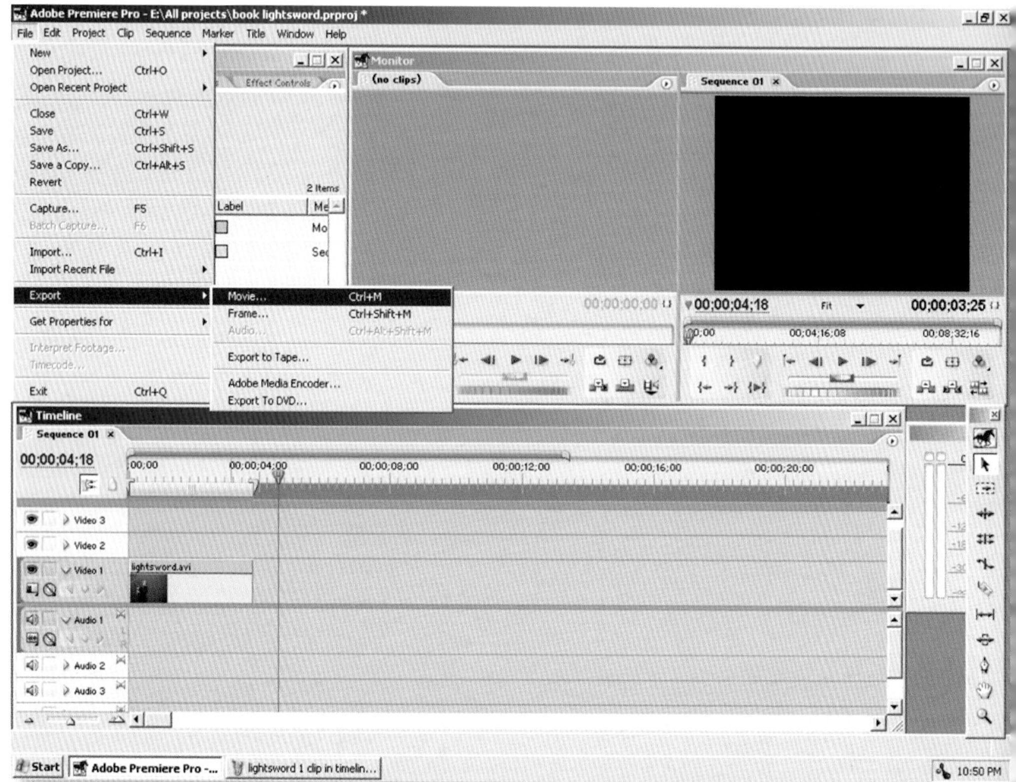

Click on **File**, **Export**, **Movie**.

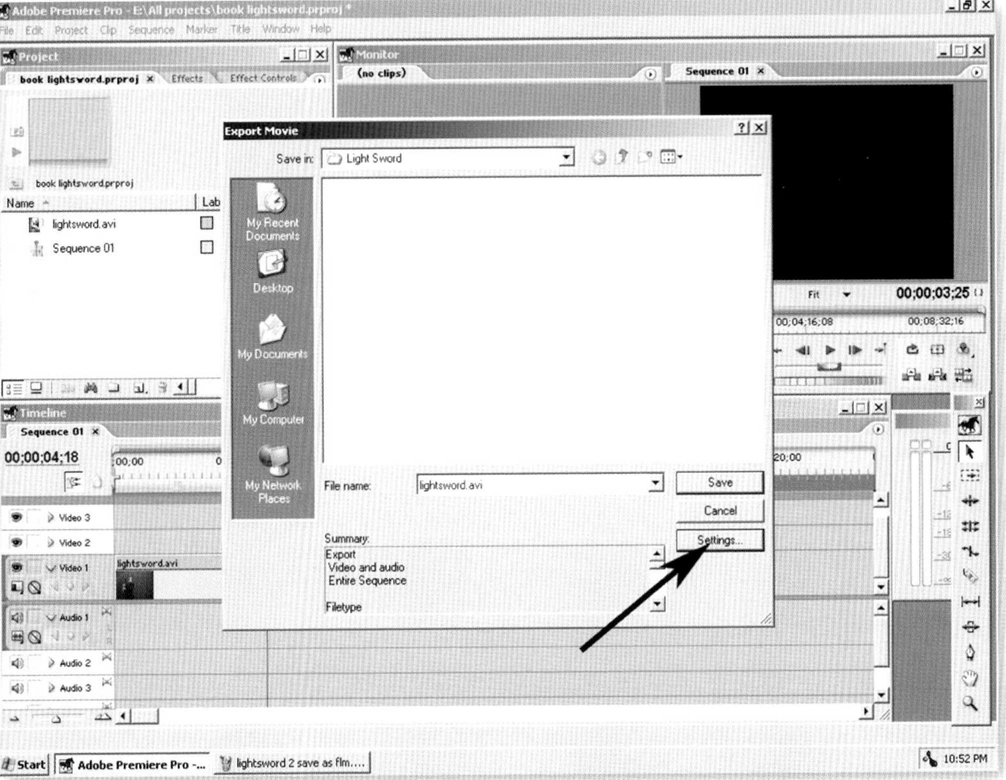

Click on **Settings**.

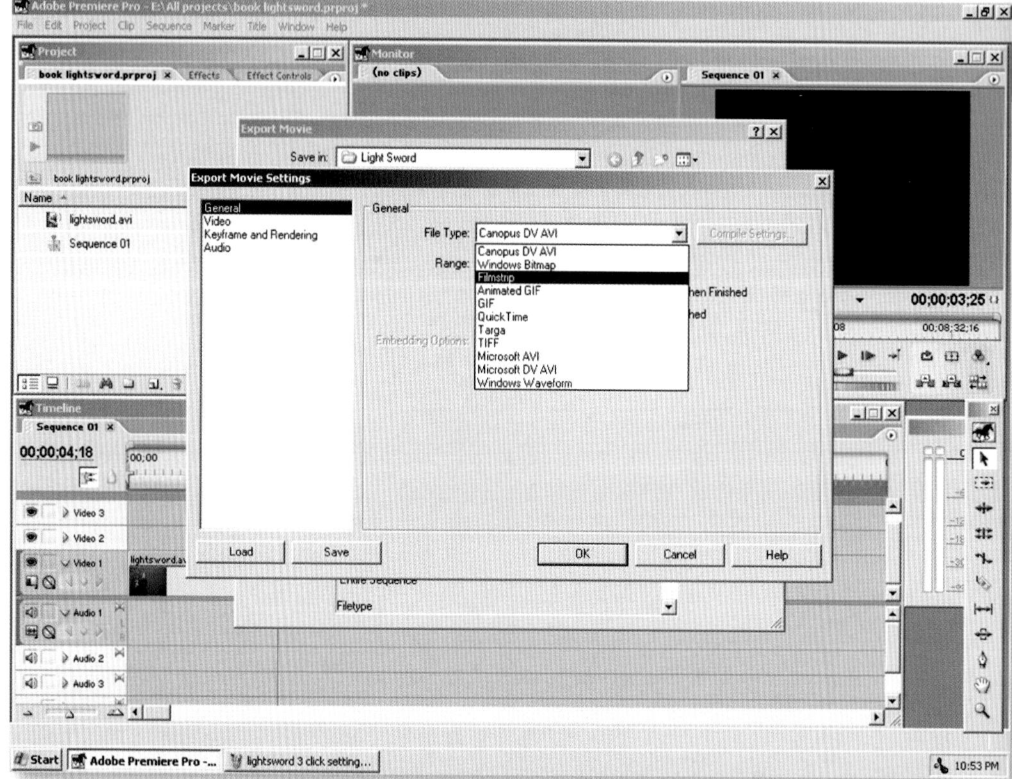

From the drop-down menu, click on **Filmstrip**.

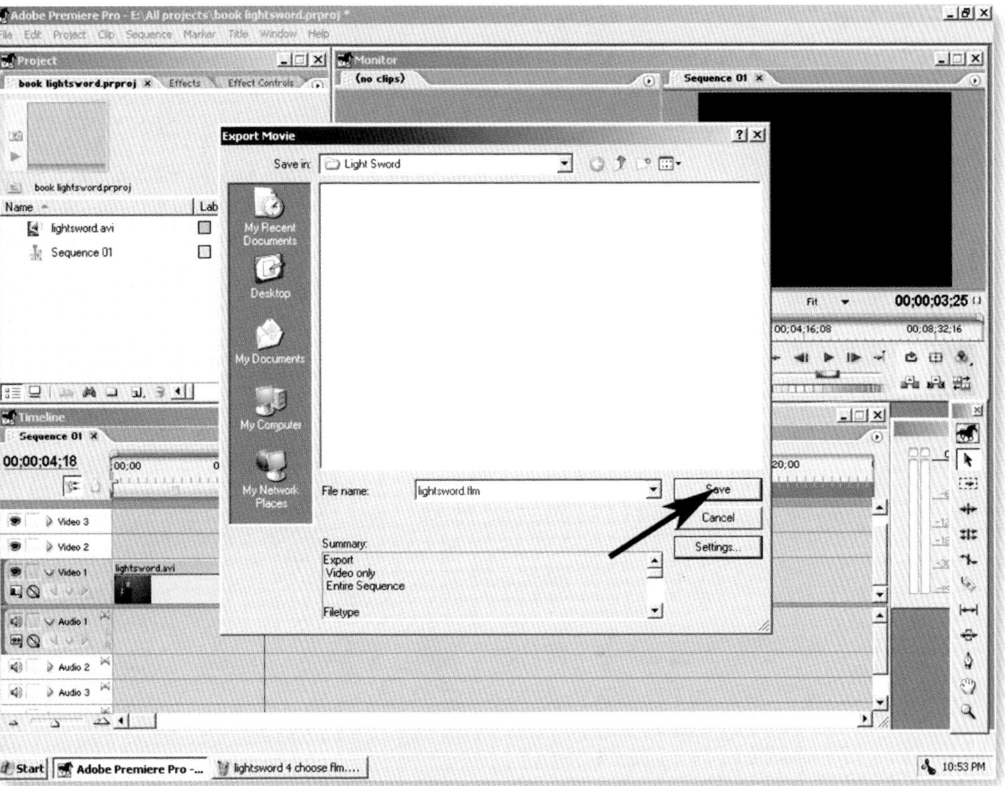

In the **File name:** field, type the name of your file. In the example above, we used the name **lightsword.flm**. Click on **Save**.

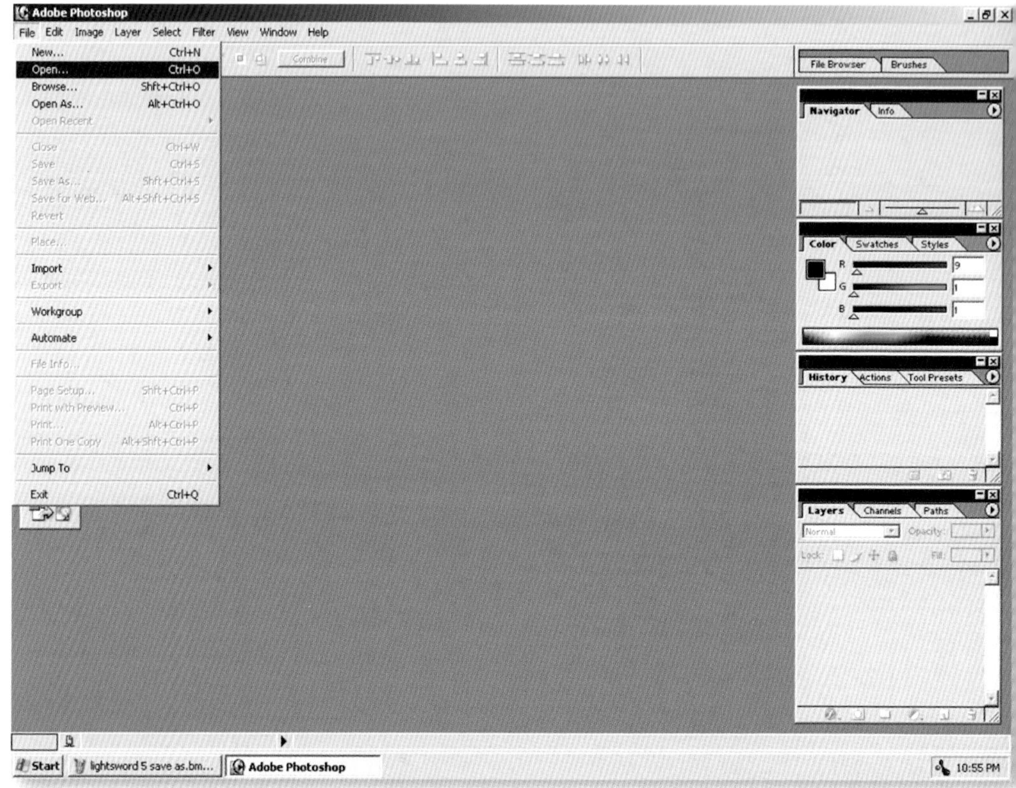

Start the program **Adobe Photoshop**. Click on **File**, **Open**.

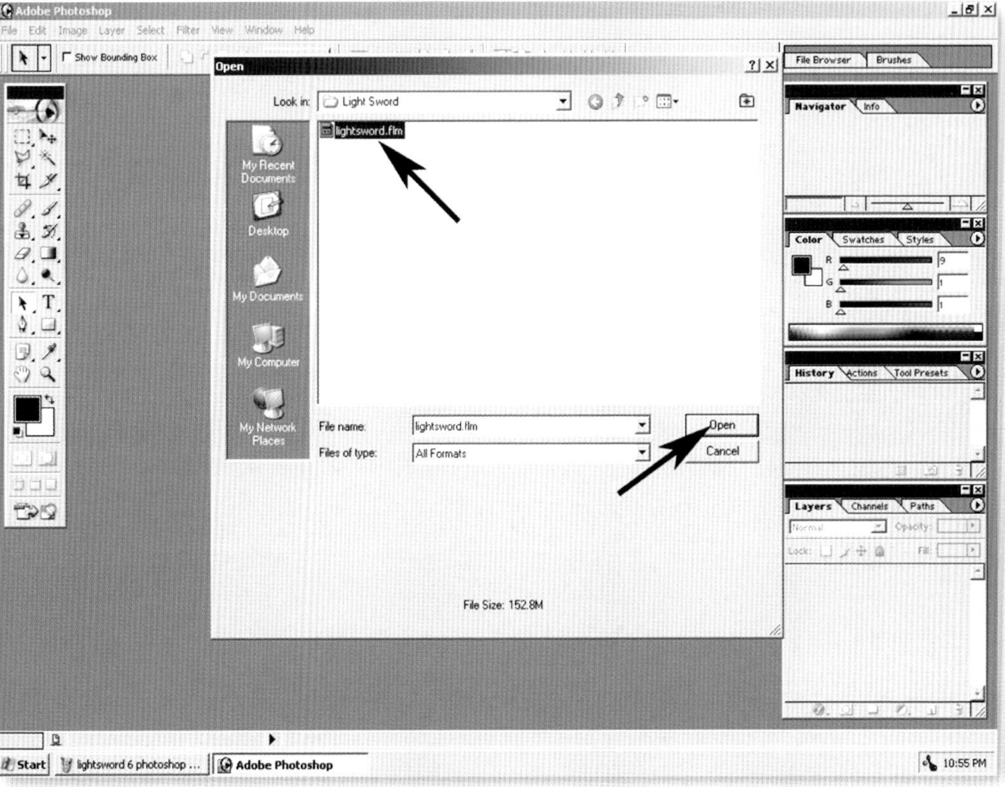

Highlight your file. In the above example, the file is called **lightsword. flm**. Click on **Open**.

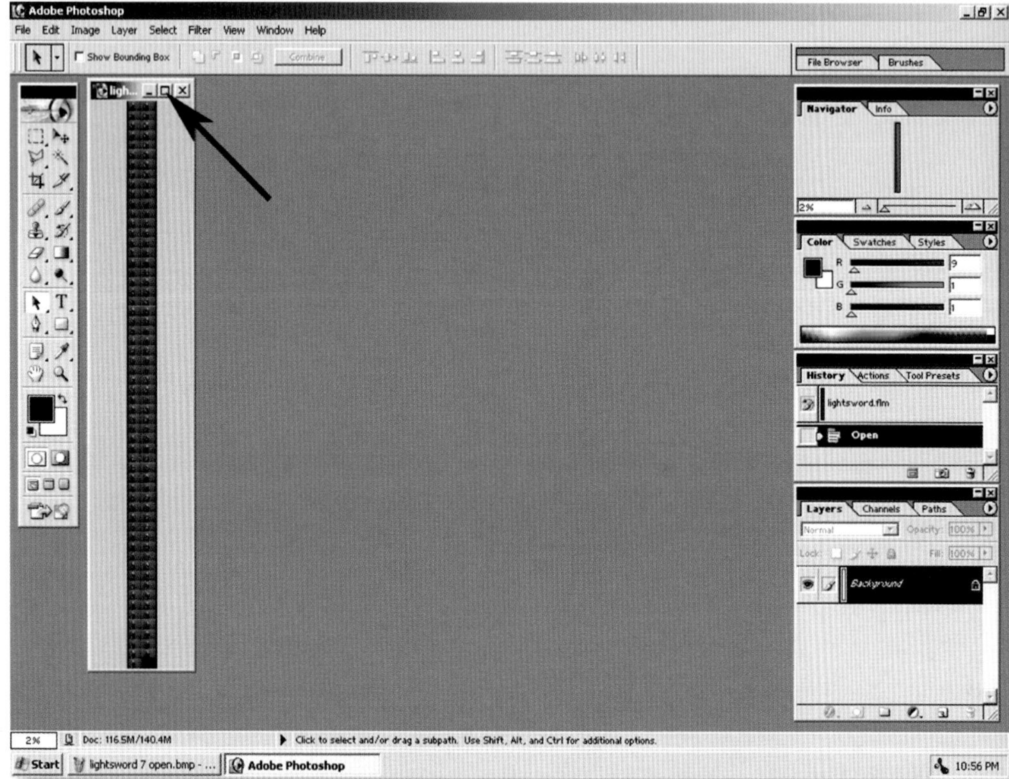

Click on the **Maximize** button.

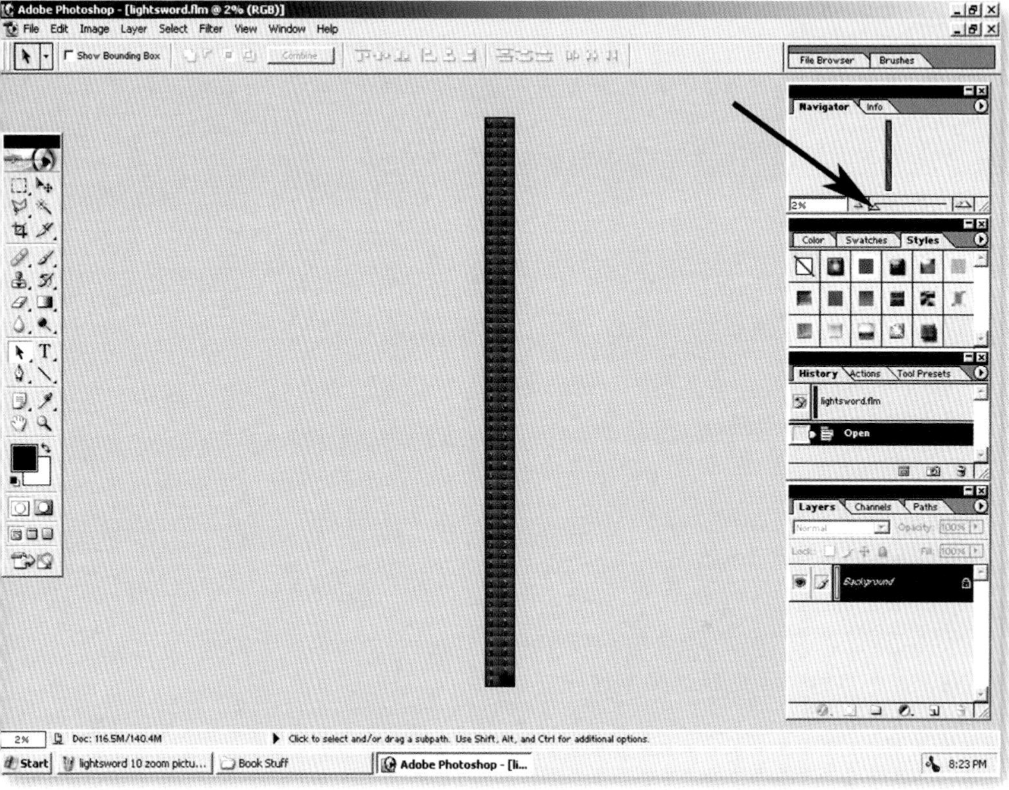

Click and drag the small triangle to the right. This will zoom in on your video clip.

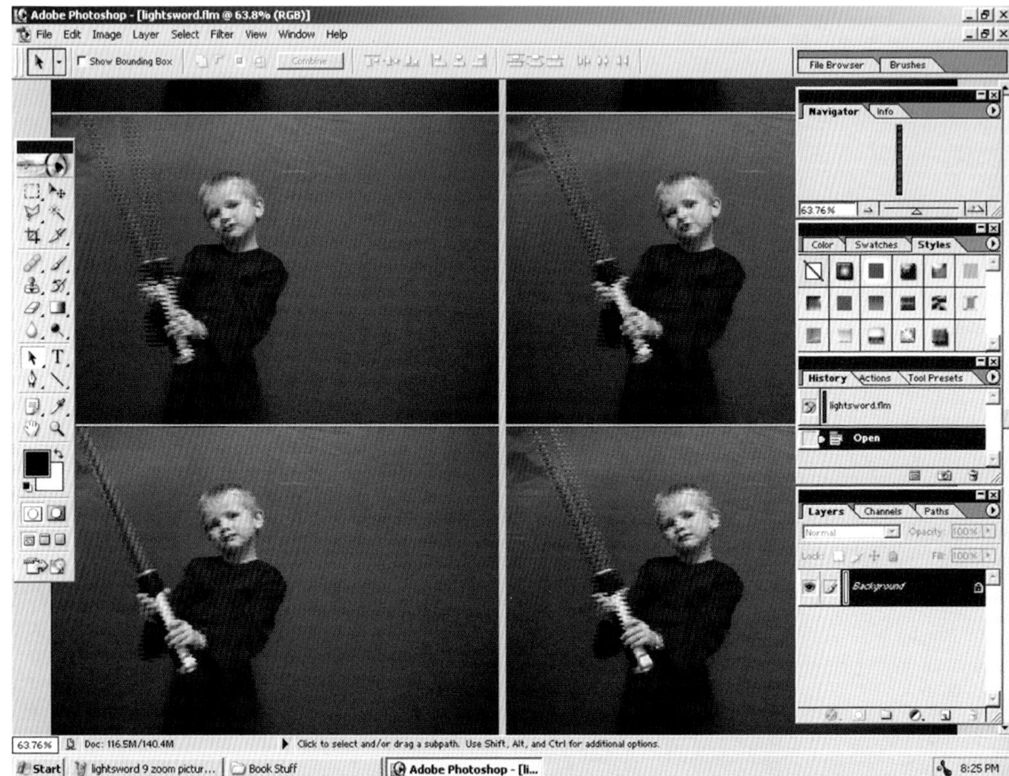

Zoom in until you can easily see the frames of your video clip. In the example above, some of the frames seem to show two Light Swords. This is because the Light Sword was moving very fast when this video was created.

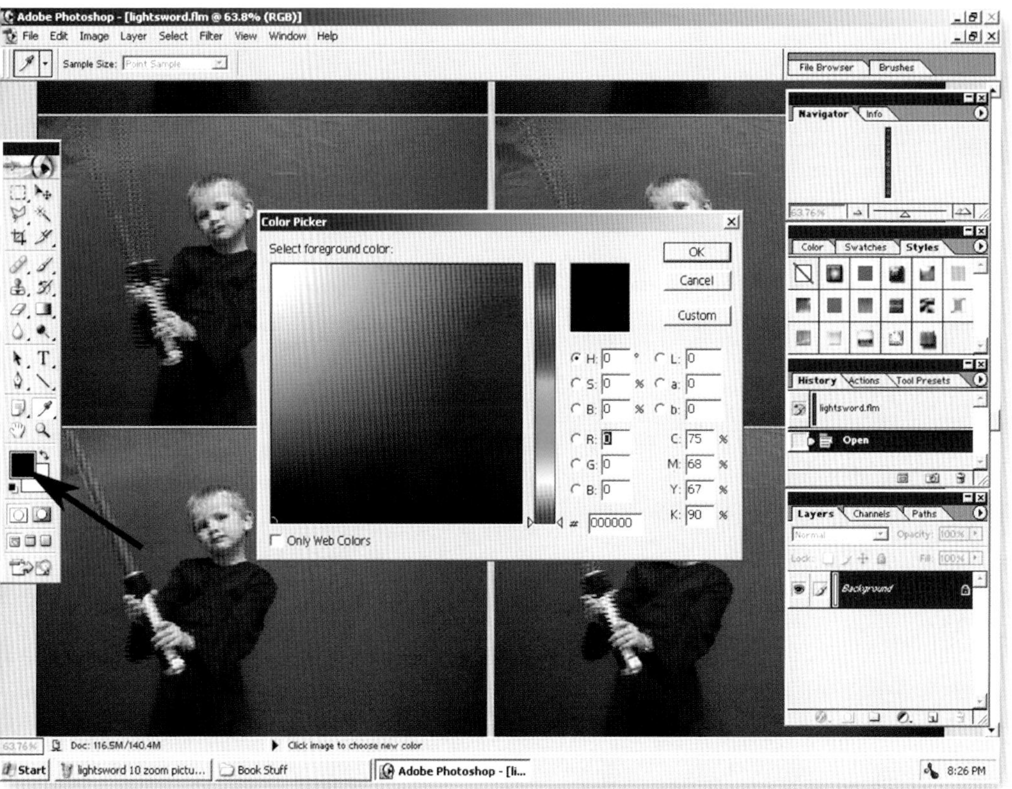

Click on the **Color Picker**.

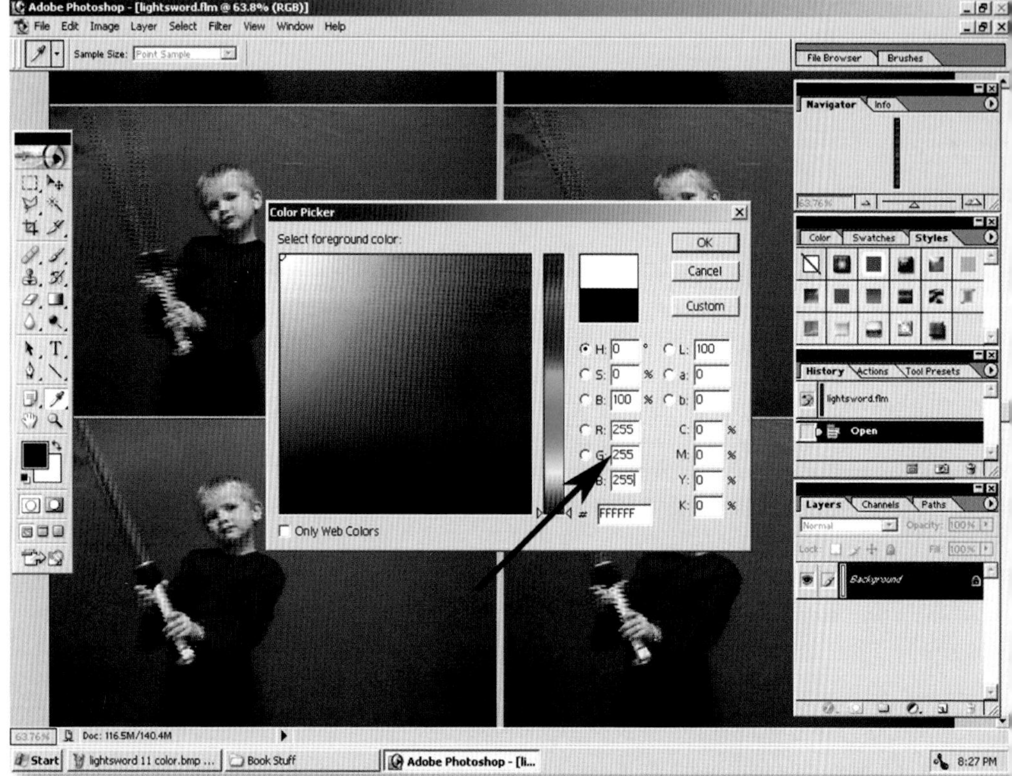

Change the numbers in the **R:**, **G:** and **B:** fields to 255. Click **OK**. This will change the color to white.

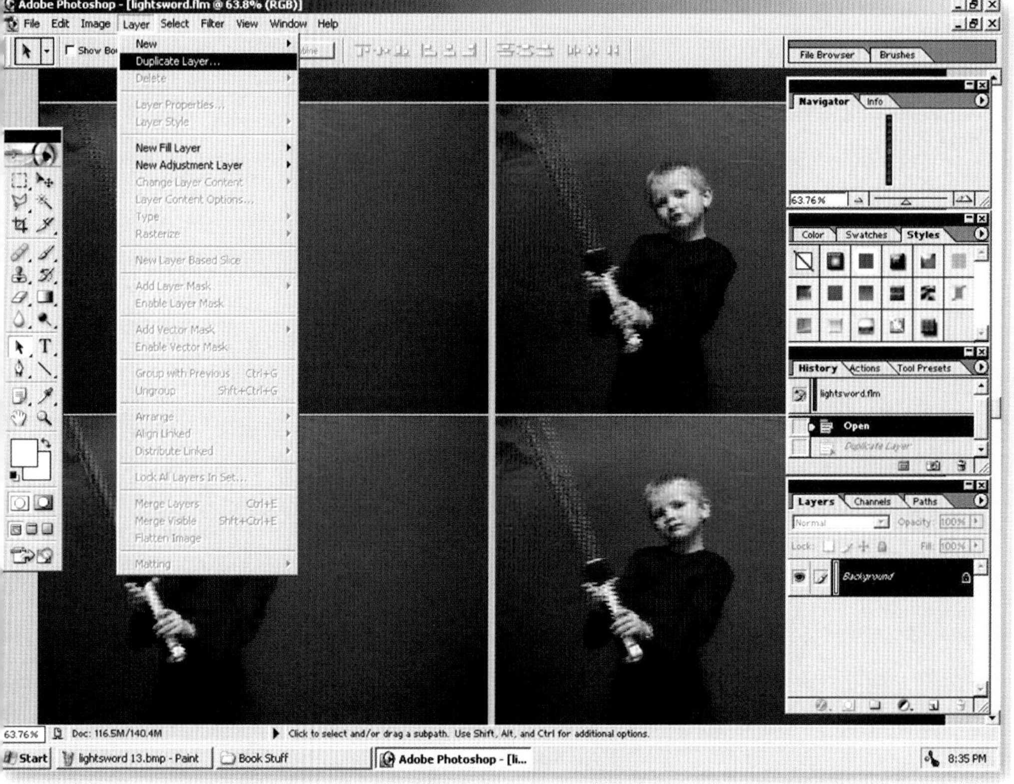

Click on **Layer**, **Duplicate Layer**.

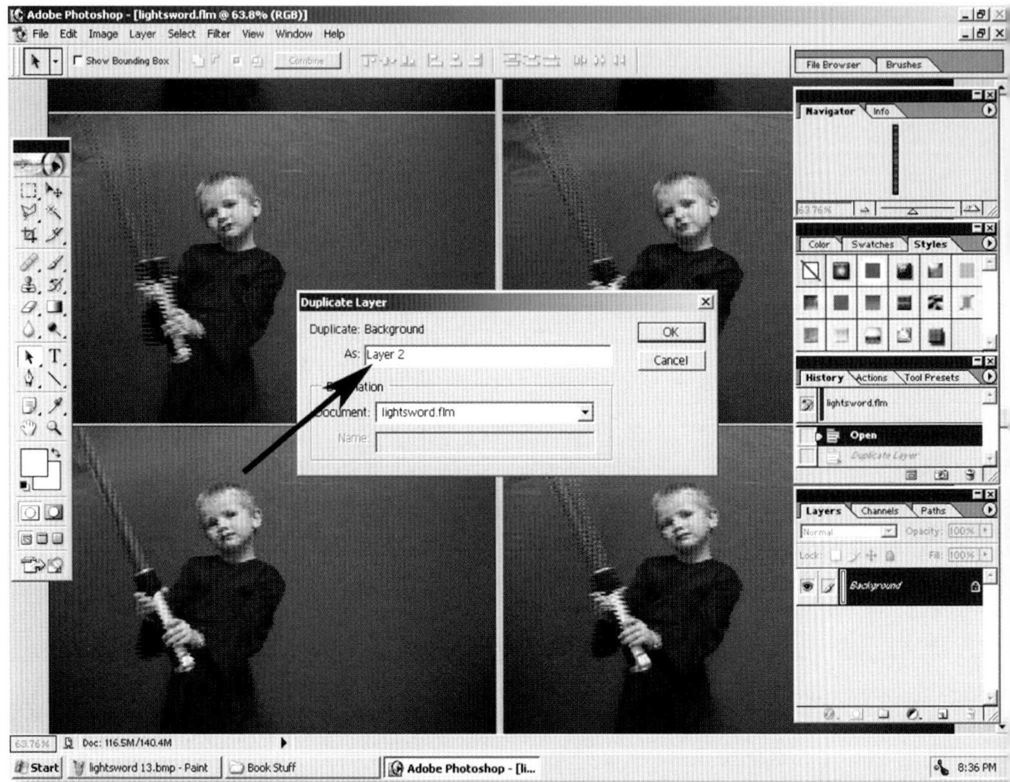

In the **As:** field, type **Layer 2**. Click **OK**.

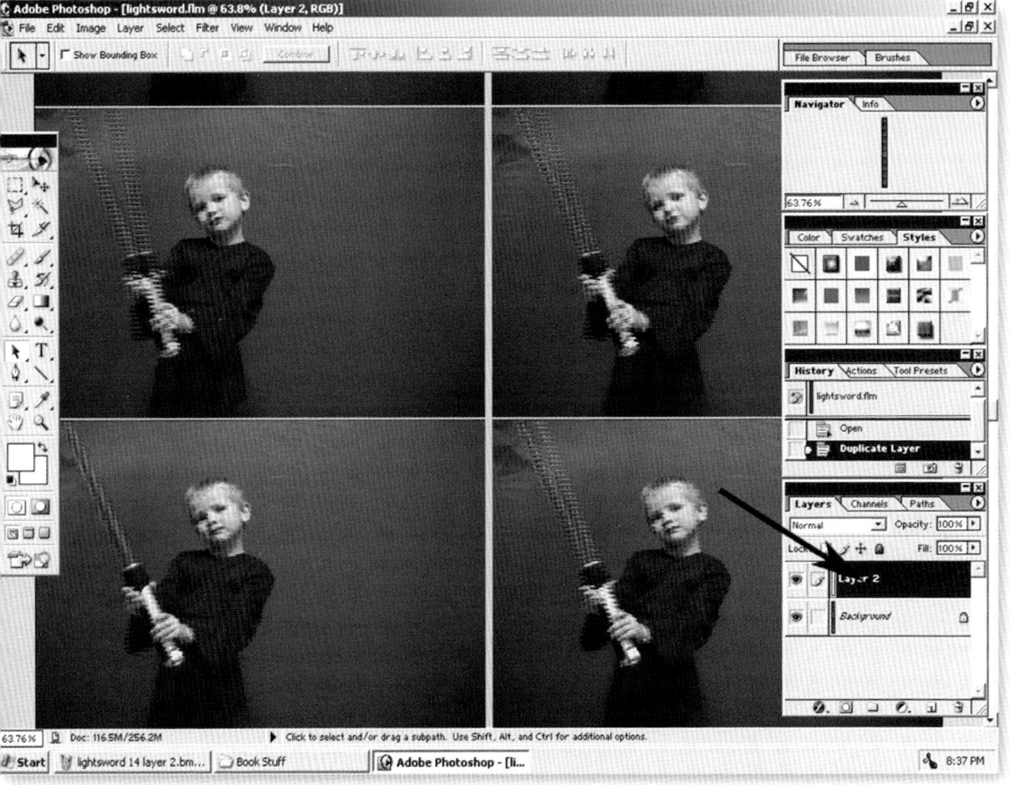

This box shows you what layers you have. Also, the layer you are working on will be highlighted.

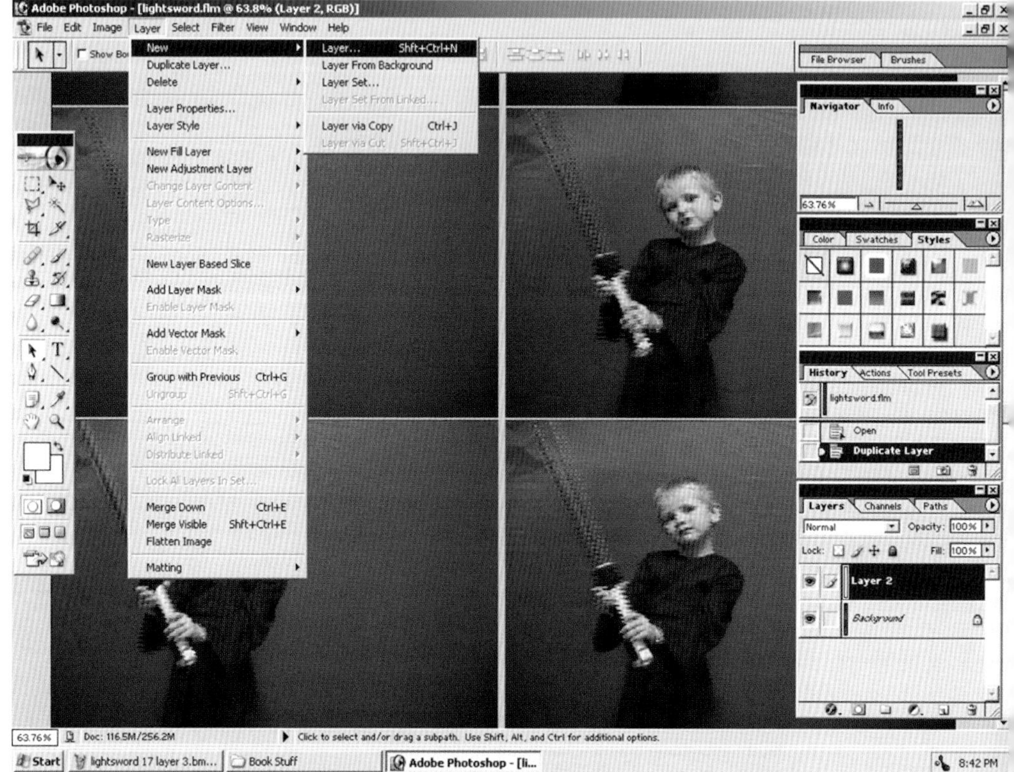

Click on **Layer**, **New**, **Layer**.

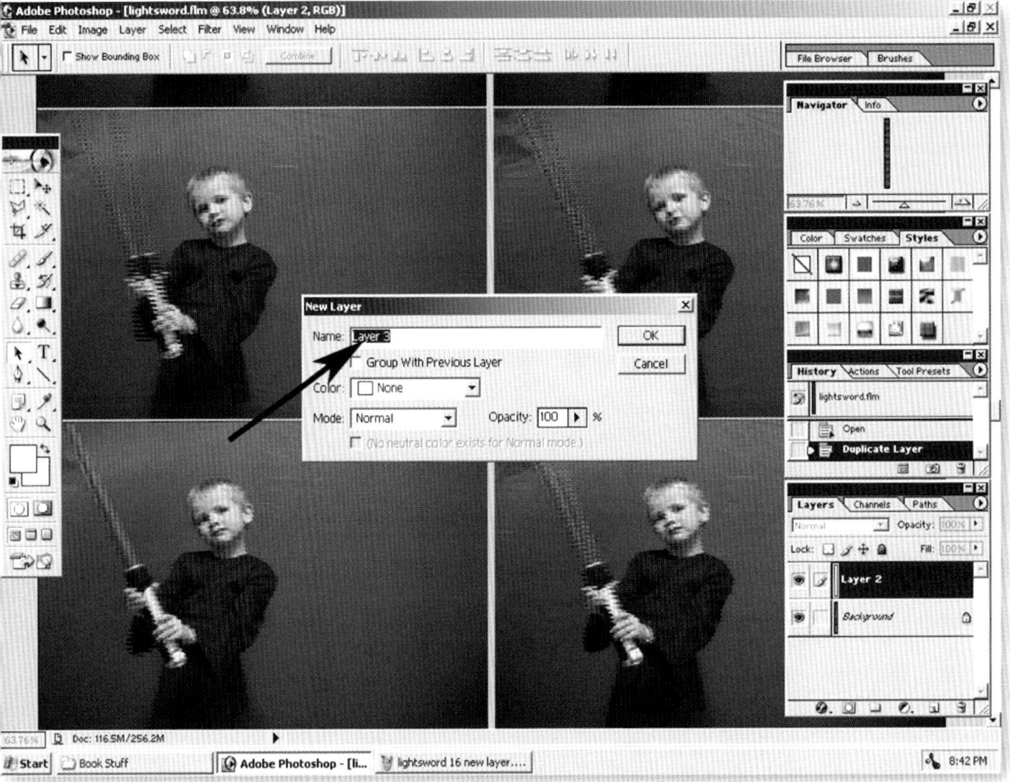

In the **Name:** field, type **Layer 3**. Click **OK**.

Click on the **Polygonal Lasso** tool.

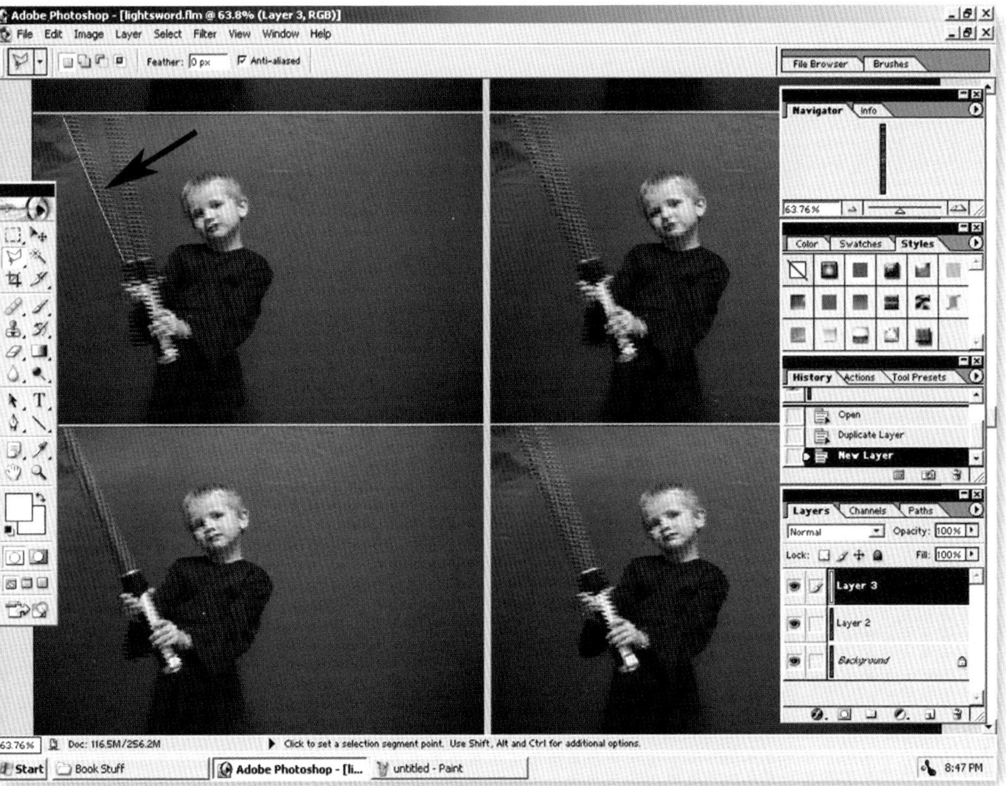

Using the **Polygonal Lasso** tool, draw a line up the left side of the Light Sword.

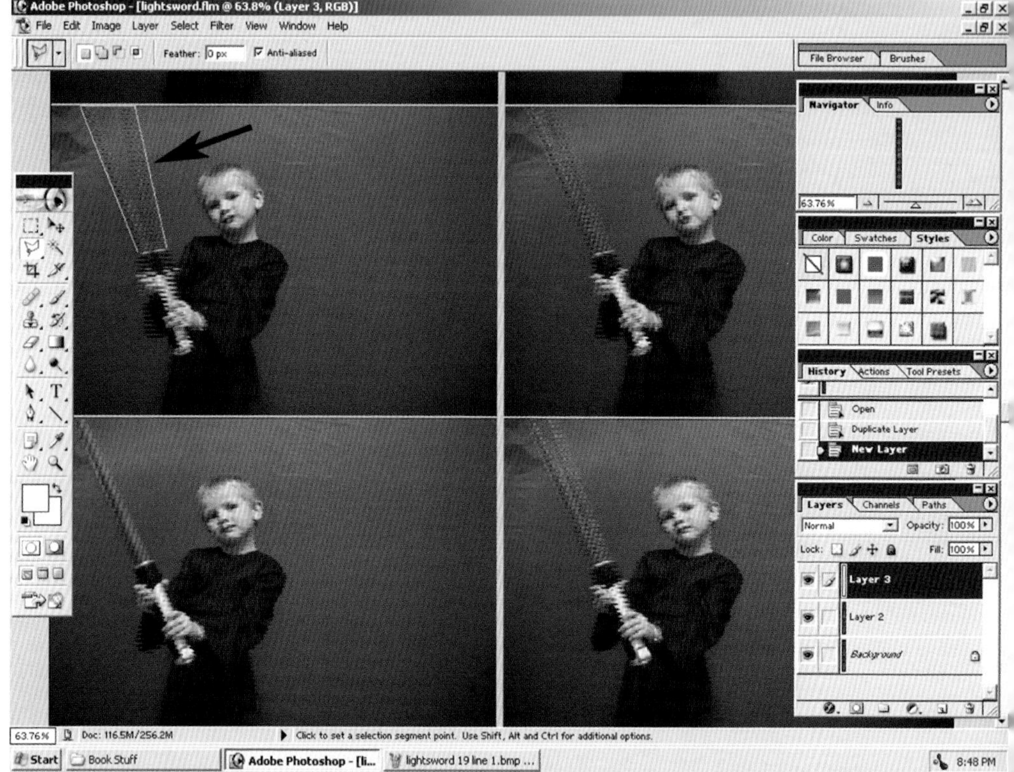

Continue drawing the line across the top and down the right side of the Light Sword.

Continue drawing the line across the bottom to completely surround the blade of the Light Sword.

Click on **Edit**, **Fill**.

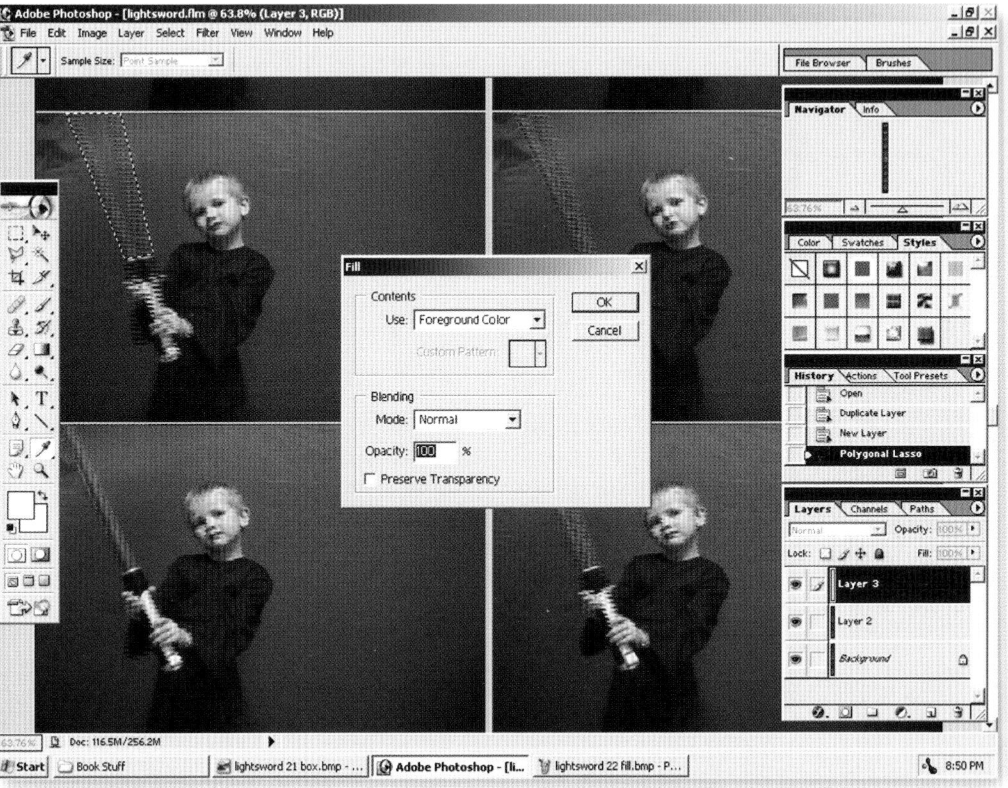
Adobe Photoshop - [lightsword.flm @ 63.8% (Layer 3, RGB)]
File Edit Image Layer Select Filter View Window Help
Sample Size:
File Browser
Brushes
Navigator
Info
Color
Swatches
Styles
History
Actions
Tool Presets
Open
Duplicate Layer
New Layer
Polygonal Lasso
Layers
Channels
Paths
Opacity:
Lock:
Fill:
Layer 3
Layer 2
Background
Fill
Contents
Use: Foreground Color
Custom Pattern:
OK
Cancel
Blending
Mode: Normal
Opacity: 100 %
Preserve Transparency
Doc: 116.5M/256.2M
Start
Book Stuff
lightsword 21 box.bmp - ...
Adobe Photoshop - [li...
lightsword 22 fill.bmp - P...
8:50 PM

Click **OK**.

This covers the blade of the Light Sword with white.

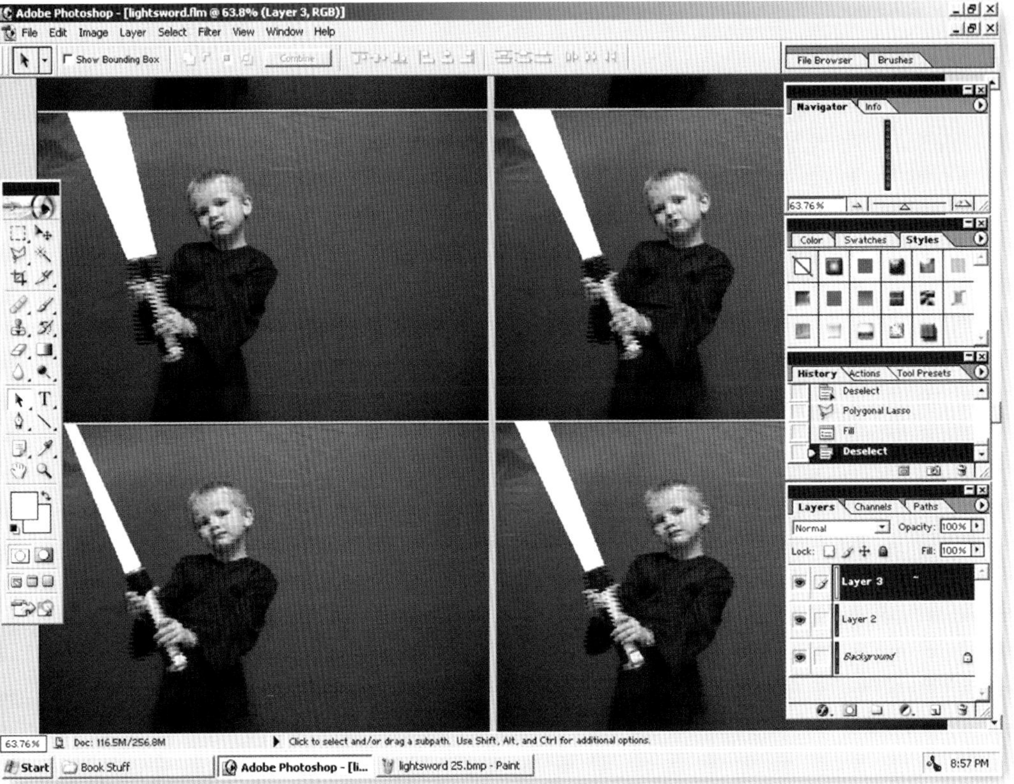

This is the most time-consuming part of the entire process. You must now repeat the process of covering the blade of the Light Sword with white on every frame of the video clip.

Click on **Layer 2**.

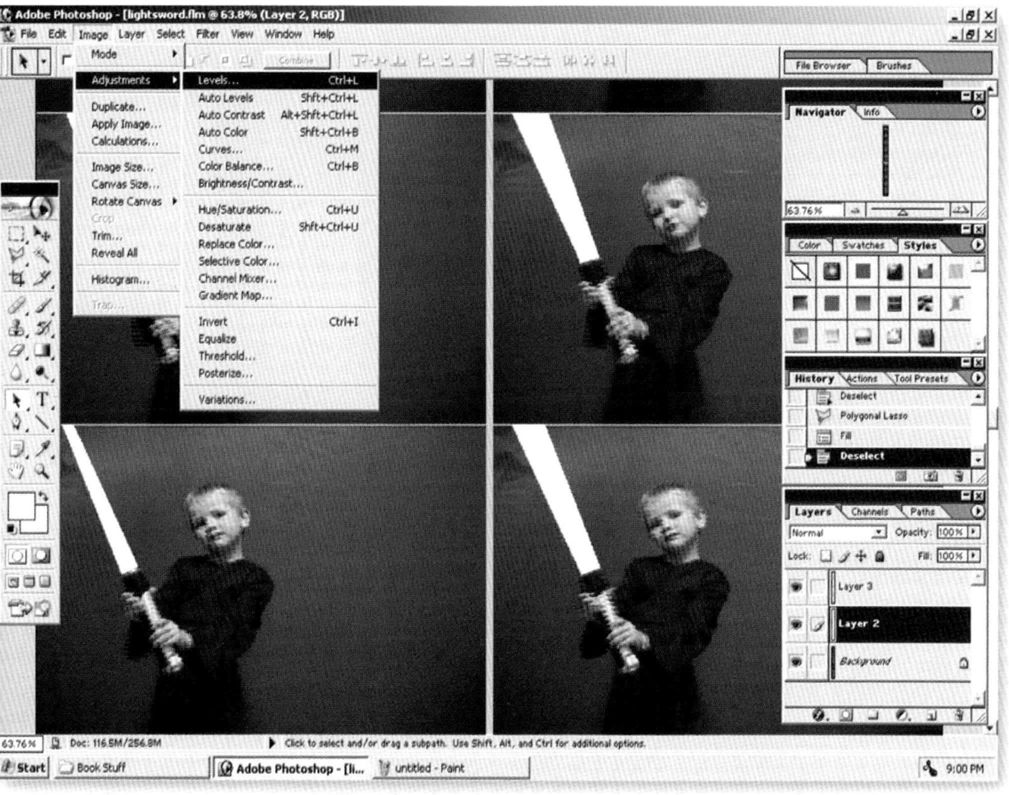

Click on **Image**, **Adjustments**, **Levels**.

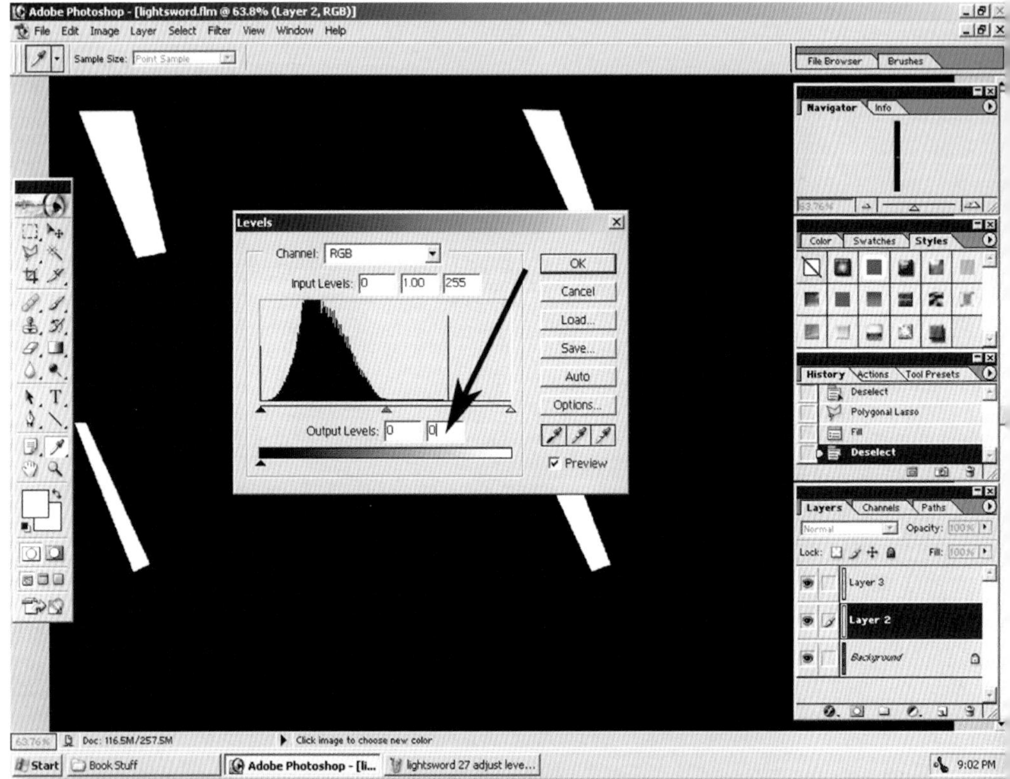

Change the right **Output Level** to **0**. Click **OK**.

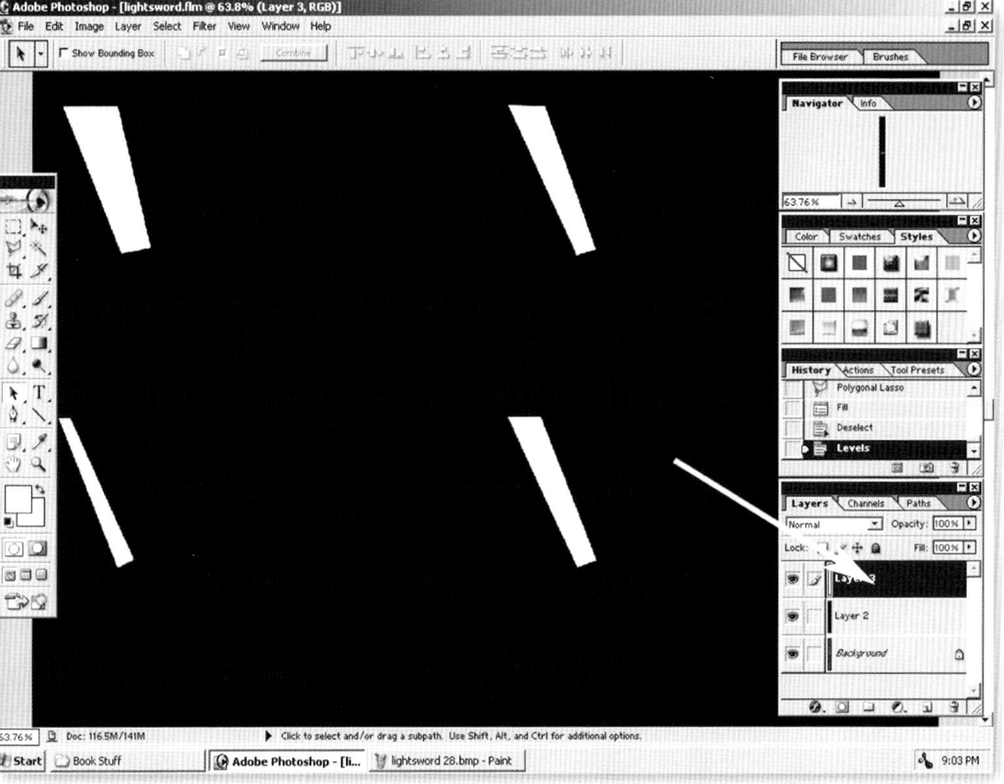

Click on **Layer 3**.

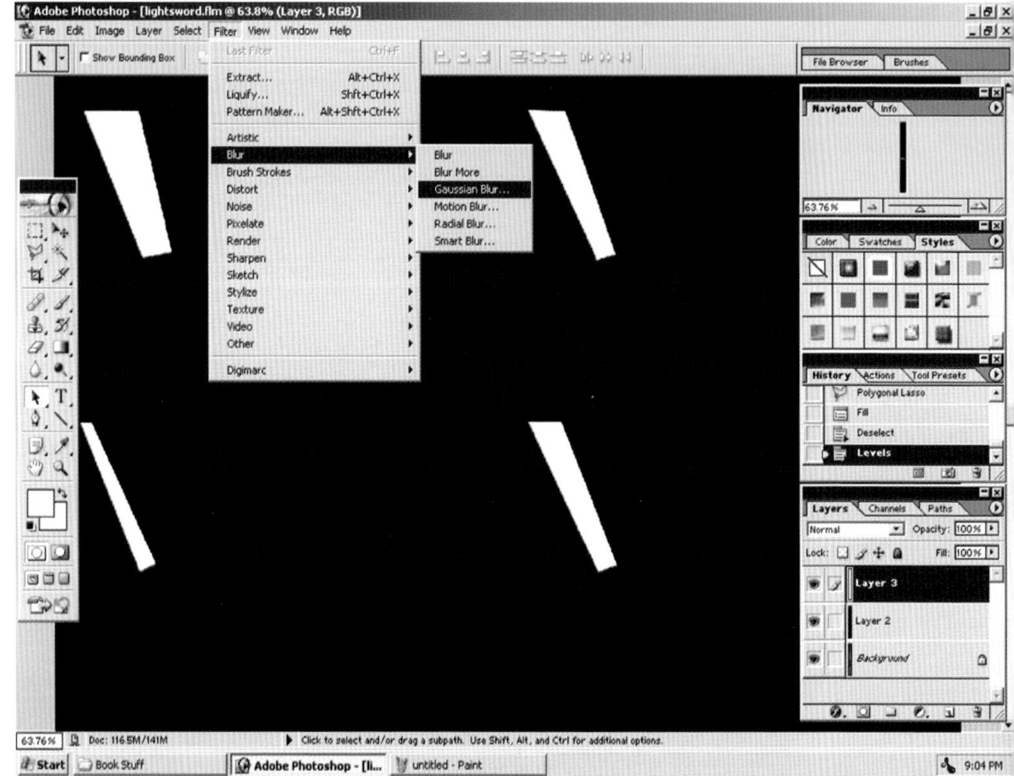

Click on **Filter**, **Blur**, **Gaussian Blur**.

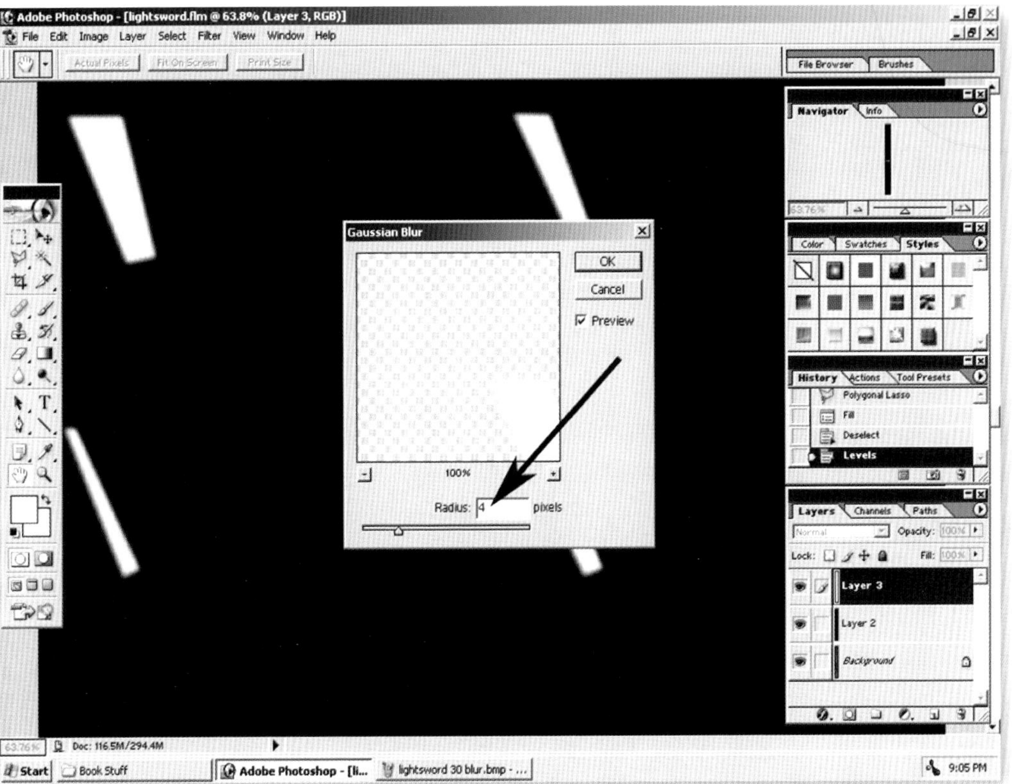

In the **Radius:** field, type in **4**. Click **OK**.

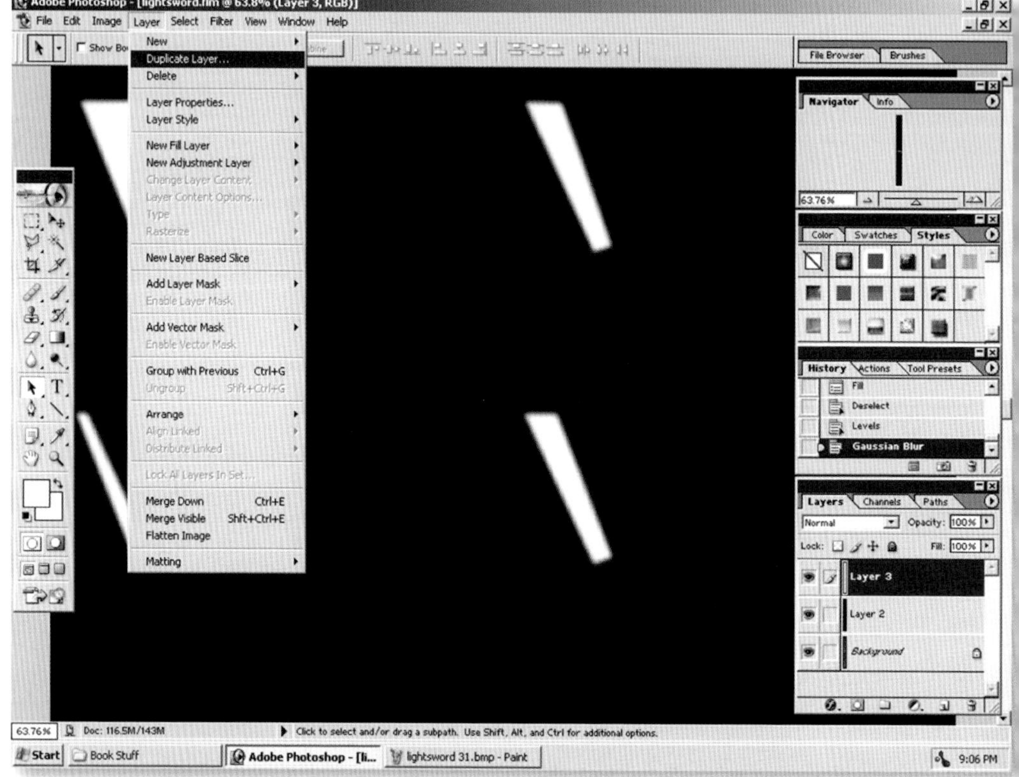

Click on **Layer**, **Duplicate Layer**.

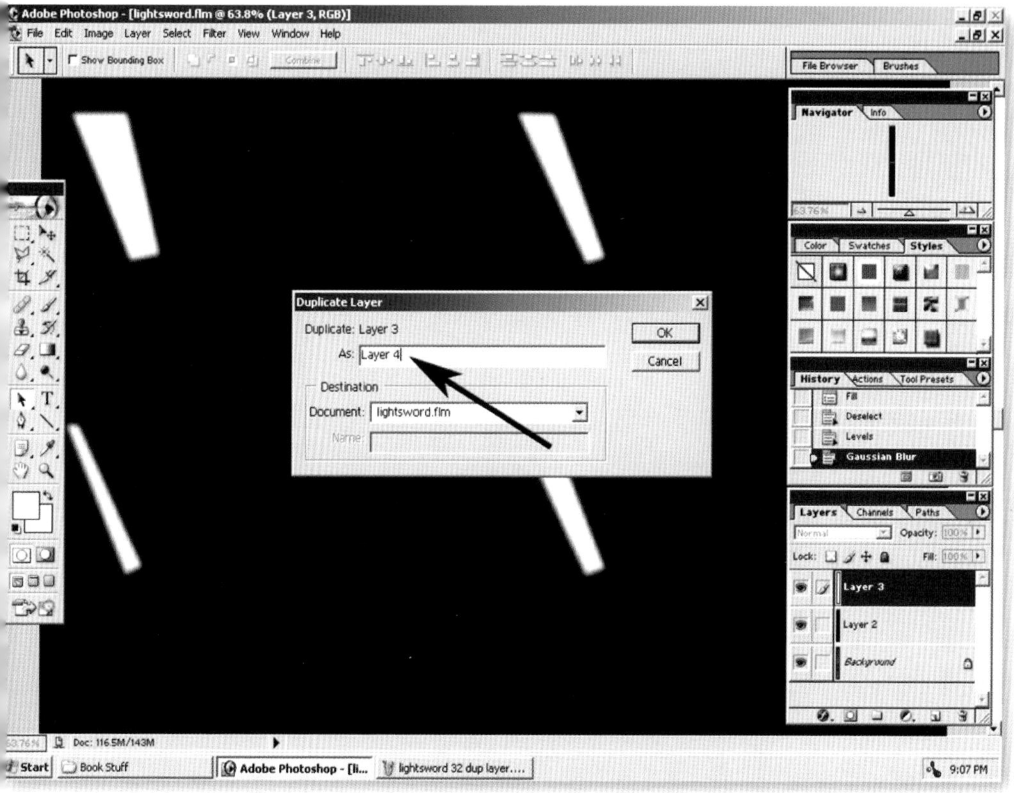

In the **As:** field, type **Layer 4**. Click **OK**.

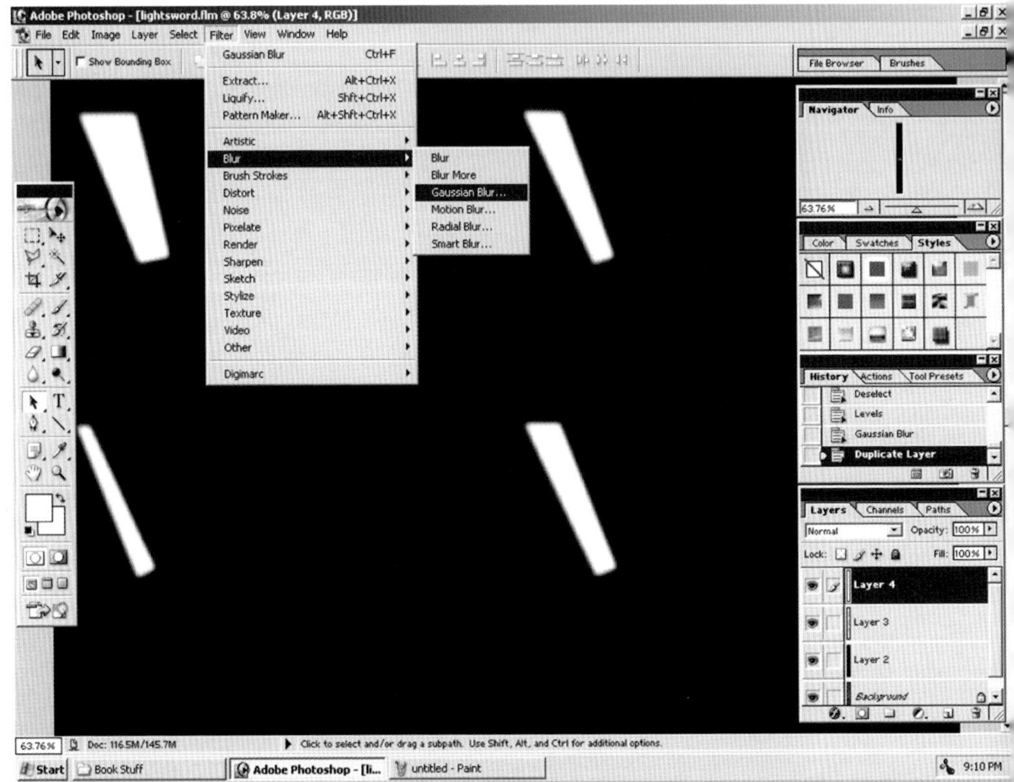

Click on **Filter**, **Blur**, **Gaussian Blur**.

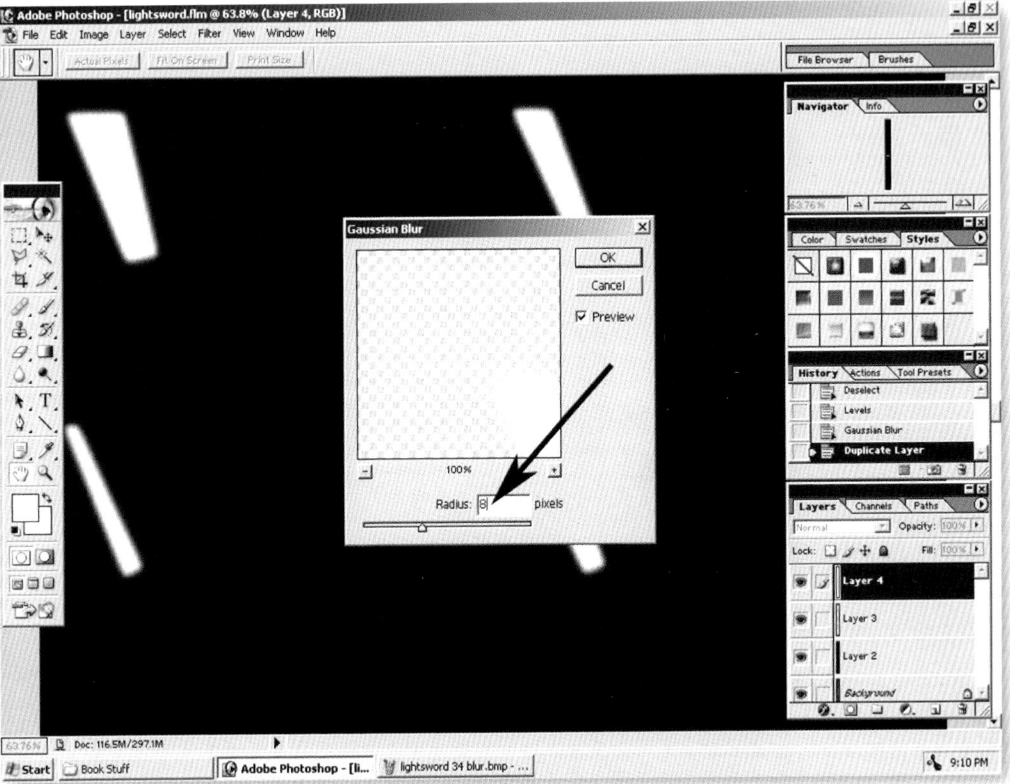

In the **Radius:** field, type **8**. Click **OK**.

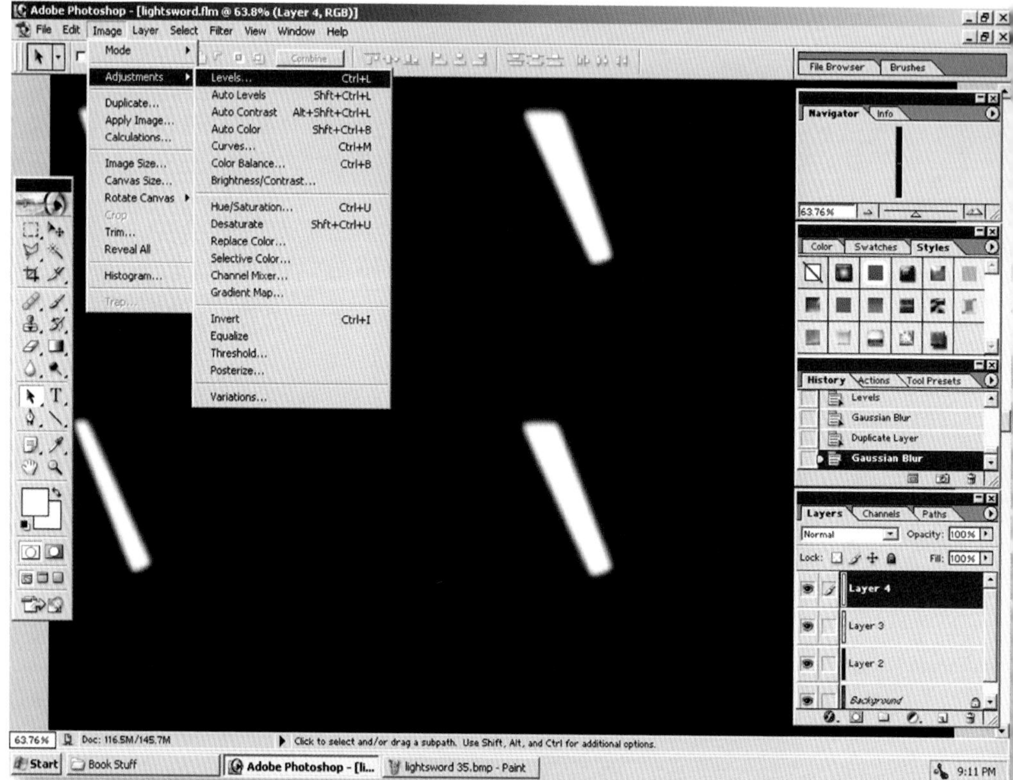

Click on **Image**, **Adjustments**, **Levels**.

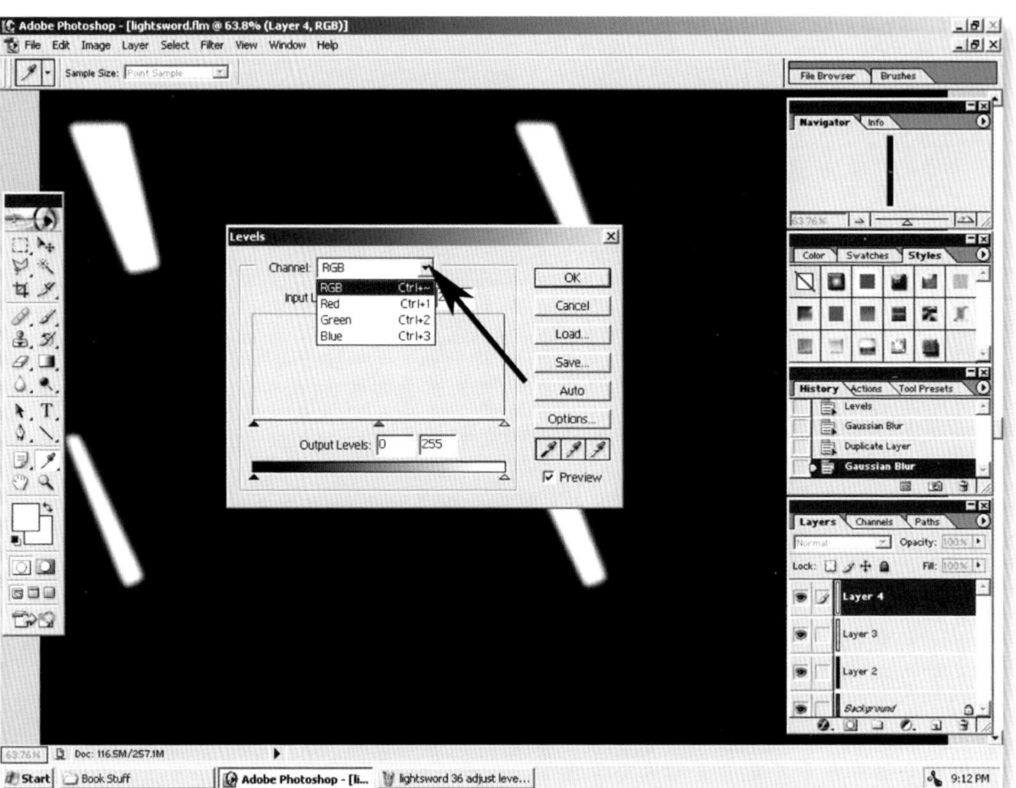

Click on the drop-down menu.

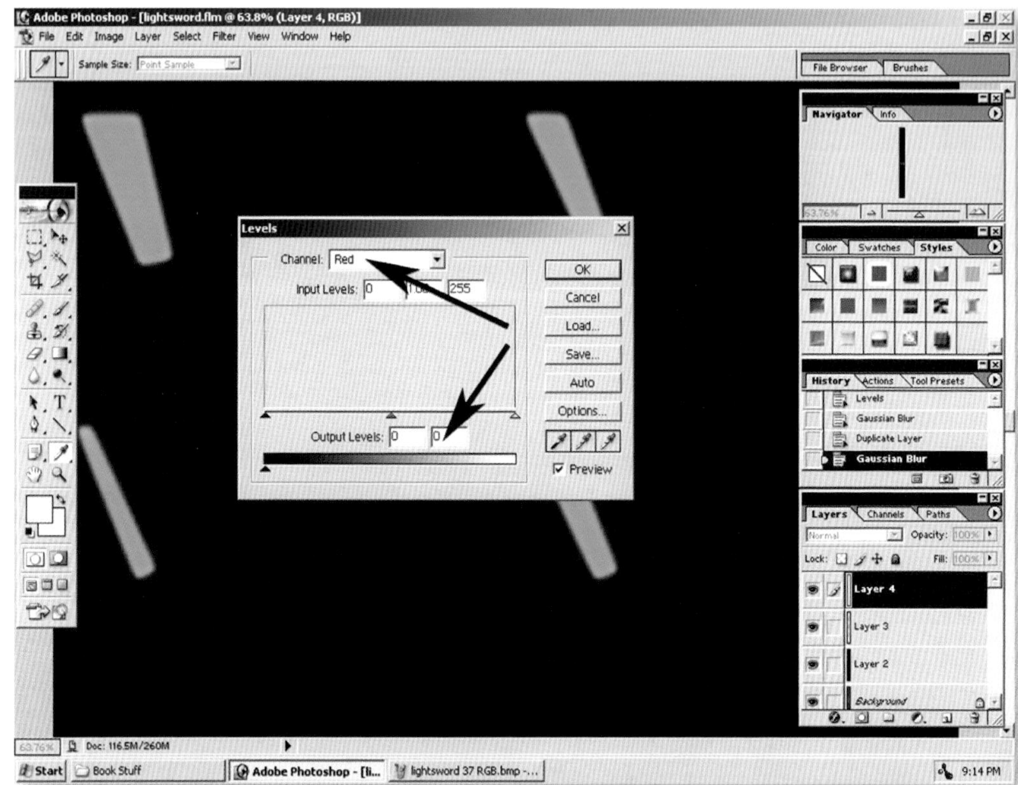

In the **Channel:** field, select **Red**. Change the right **Output Level** to **0**.

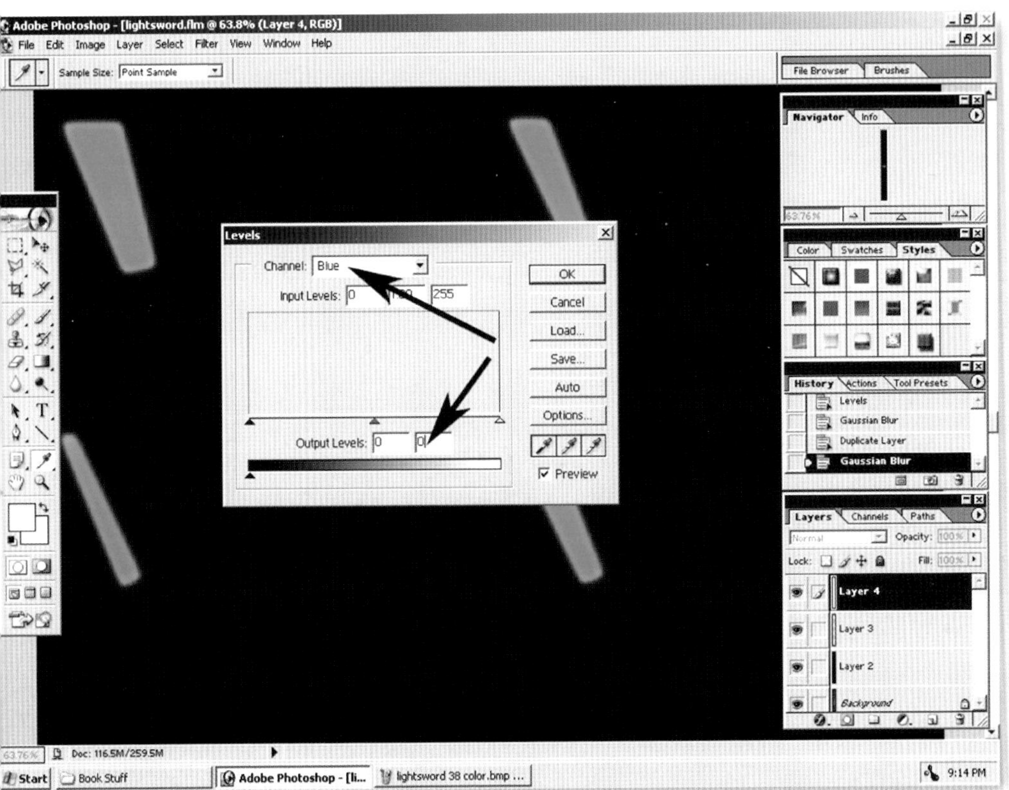

In the **Channel:** field, select **Blue**. Change the right **Output Level** to **0**. This will change the color of your Light Sword to green. You can choose different colors by changing the right **Output Level** for the **Red**, **Blue** and **Green Channels**. Click **OK**.

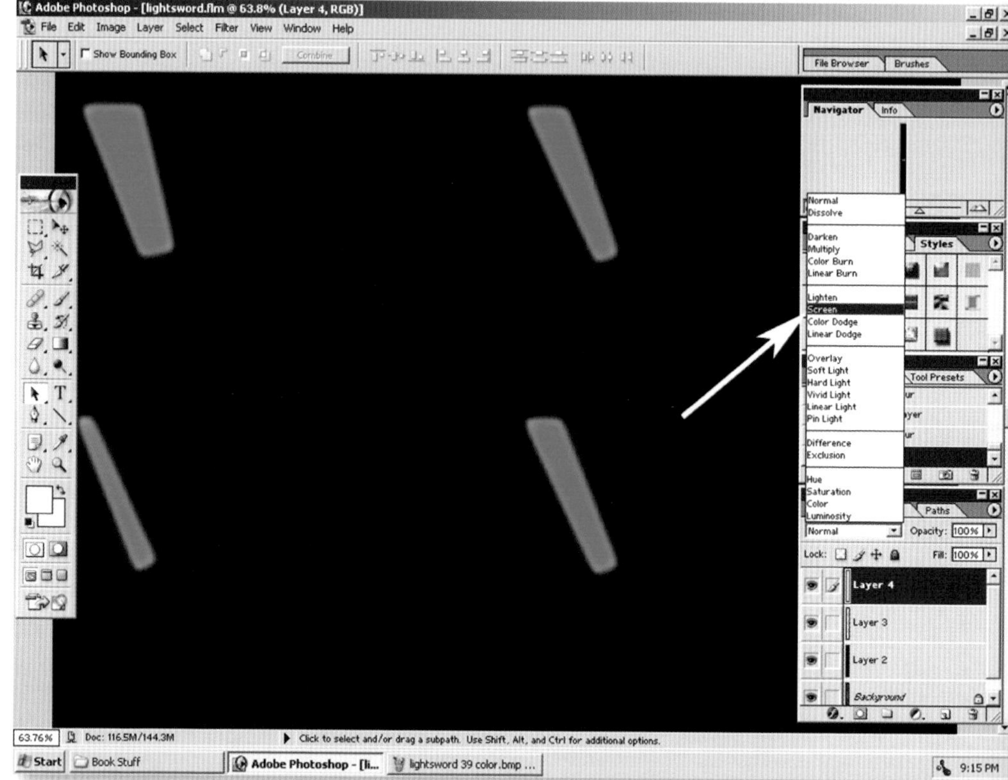

Click on **Screen** from the drop-down menu.

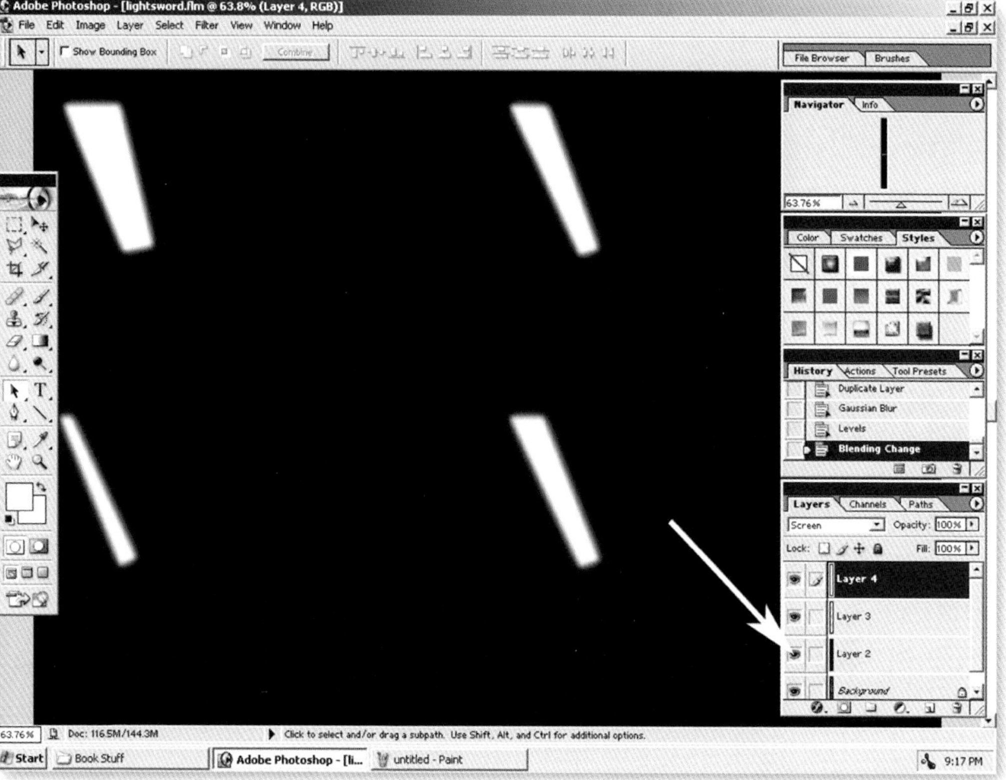

Click on the little eye next to **Layer 2**. This will cause the little eye to disappear.

This is what the final effect will look like.

Click on **Layer**, **Flatten Image**.

Click **OK**.

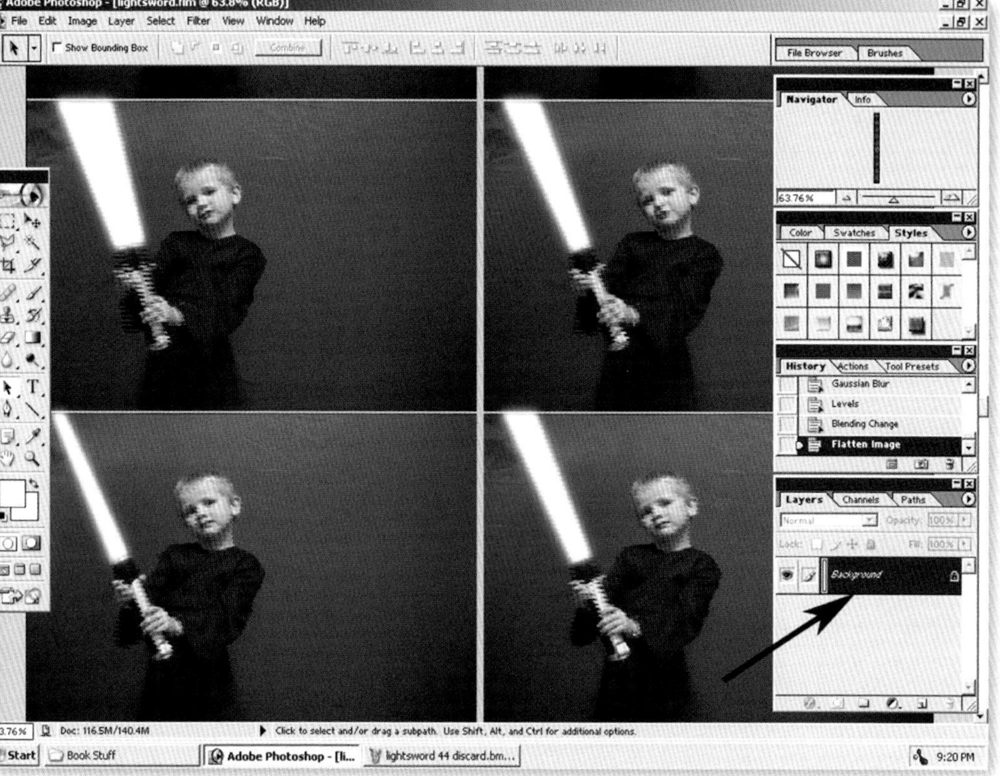

After you flatten the image, there is only one layer called **Background**.

Click on **File**, **Save As**.

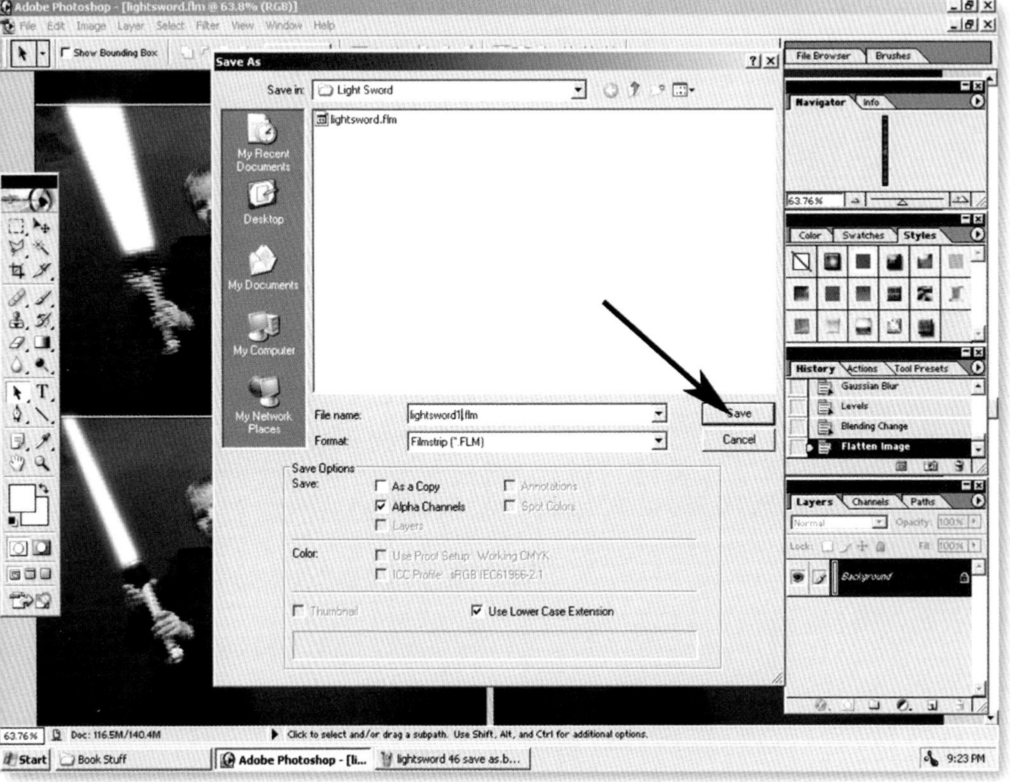

In the **File name:** field, type **lightsword1.flm**. Click **Save**. You can now open up **Adobe Premiere Pro** and import your edited video clip.

SECTION 16

STOCK FOOTAGE

What do you do if you need a shot flying though Los Angeles in a helicopter, or you need a shot of a shark swimming right by your camera? Some shots are just too dangerous or too expensive to get. If all else fails, you can consider buying "Stock Footage." These are shots that you can buy and use in your movies royalty-free. You can find just about any type of shot you could want. (Not all stock footage is royalty-free; some companies license, and price, footage according to use.) There are several companies that sell royalty-free stock footage, but one of the more popular of these companies is **Art Beats**. Their website is **www.artbeats.com**. Or you can just type in "stock footage" into your favorite web browser. Stock footage can be expensive, sometimes priced at hundreds of dollars per shot. Other times you can get a whole CD of shots for much less. You can get everything from fire, rain and thunderstorms, to oceans, mountains and everything in between. Stock footage can add a professional touch to your movies, and might just take your production to the next level.

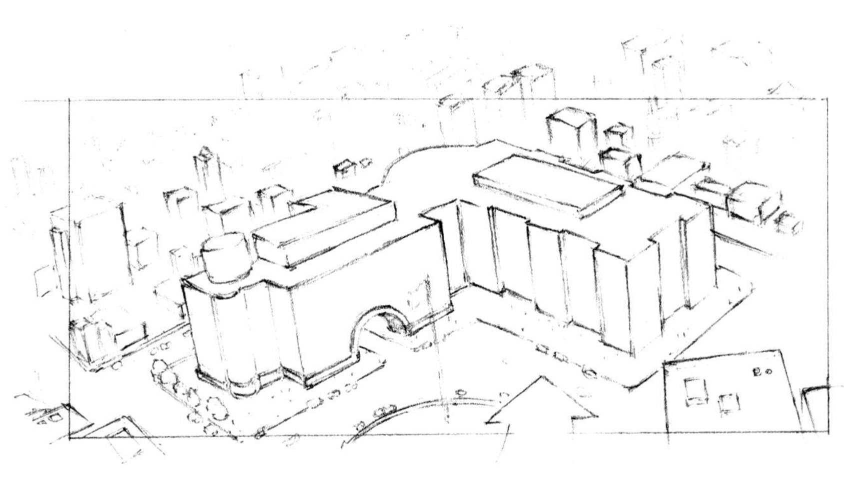

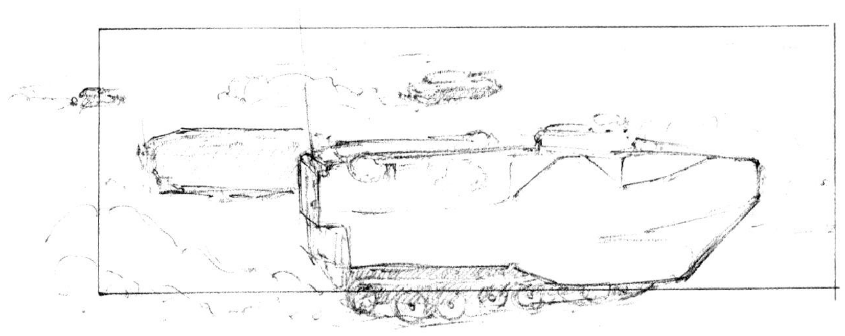

STOCK FOOTAGE COMPANIES

Here are some companies that offer stock footage for almost any situation or occasion.

Artbeats
www.artbeats.com
(800) 444-9392
Types of footage: Aerials, Animals, Animation, Imagery, Backgrounds, Education, Effects, Establishments, Lifestyles, Medical, Military, Nature, Science, Sports, Travel

Digital Juice, Inc.
www.digitaljuice.com
(800) 525-2203
Types of footage: Aerials, Animals, Animation, Health, History, Imagery, Landscapes, Military, Music, Nature, Ocean, Science, Sports, Travel

Buyout Footage
www.buyoutfootage.com
(714) 693-1250
Types of footage: Animation, Disasters, Education, Effects, History, Imagery, Lifestyle, Medical, Military, Nature, Science, Sports, Travel, Weather

Digital Hotcakes
www.digitalhotcakes.com
(866) 745-7334
Types of footage: Aerials, Animation, Landscapes, Lifestyles, Marine Life, Medical, Nature, Travel

SECTION 17

FXhome

FXhome was formed in early 2001 by Joshua Davies and Toby Walsh. Their aim was to provide low-budget and enthusiast filmmakers with the means to create blockbuster special effects. The first step towards this goal was the creation of a computer program called **AlamDV**, which began life as a simple lightsaber effects program, but was soon expanded into a fully featured visual effects tool. Additional staff joined **FXhome** in 2002 to help develop future products.

In 2006, FXhome moved into new territory after three years of intensive research and development, resulting in the simultaneous release of **EffectsLab**, **CompositeLab** and **VisionLab Studio**. These FXhome products now cover computer-generated visual effects, advanced compositing and digital grading, making them invaluable additions to any filmmaker's toolkit.

EffectsLab Pro makes stunning cinematic effects possible for enthusiasts and professionals alike. It features powerful tools that can create thousands of different visual effects including muzzle flashes, smoke, rain, bullet impacts, lens flares, lasers, Light Swords and much more. It also provides tools for masking, distortion, blurs and color correction. EffectsLab Pro provides Hollywood spectacle without the Hollywood budget.

CompositeLab Pro brings the power of compositing to enthusiasts and budget-conscious filmmakers. This fully featured toolkit includes everything a compositor needs: greenscreen, bluescreen, advanced keying, digital color grading, garbage mattes, animation, masking and much more.

VisionLab Studio combines all the features of EffectsLab Pro and CompositeLab Pro in a single, stand-alone package. It also includes additional filters and effects, an enhanced interface and a full commercial license.

FXhome.com has grown into one of the largest filmmaking communities on the internet with over 40,000 registered members from all over the world. Their extensive website is thriving, with a real community spirit that offers all kinds of filmmaking advice, the results of which can be seen in the online cinema. The members also seem to value the fact that they can communicate directly with the creators of the programs and even influence the development of future versions.

For more information and pricing on these products, please visit their website at **www.FXhome.com**.

SECTION 18

BLACKPOOL STUDIOS

BlackPool Studios is a company of only one employee, Eric Chauvin. He specializes in matte paintings, effects animation and compositing. He has created special effects shots for many big-budget movies and television shows, including *Star Trek: Voyager, Star Trek: Enterprise, Babylon 5, The X Files, Smallville, Alias,* the re-releases of the *Star Wars* films, *Bicentennial Man, Vertical Limit, Sleepers, Contact,* and others. He has been nominated for six Emmy awards and has won twice. The reason I wanted to showcase Eric Chauvin and his company is to show what can be done with the technology that is available today. You don't have to work at a huge company or live in Hollywood to be on the cutting edge of special effects. Eric Chauvin lives in Washington State and works completely freelance. Eric started doing matte painting work in 1991 as a traditional matte painter. This means that Eric used real paint on a surface that was shot with a real camera. By 1993, he was using **Adobe Photoshop** and has been working digitally ever since. His first job as a matte painter was at **ILM** (Industrial Light & Magic), where he was hired as an assistant matte painter for the movie *Hook*. He was then hired back again by ILM to work on *The Young Indiana Jones Chronicles.* That was supposed to be a five-week job, but he ended up staying three more years. While he was working for ILM during the day, he was moonlighting doing digital matte shots for *Babylon 5*, *Star Trek: The Next Generation* and *Star Trek: Voyager*. At the end of 1995, he decided to move to Washington State and has been there ever since. Since post-production has moved into the digital age, it is no longer necessary for visual effects companies to be located near Los Angeles. From his office in Washington, Eric works on productions from England, Australia, Canada and the United States.

The computer programs that Eric uses to create his realistic special effects are **Adobe Photoshop** for painting, **Electric Image** for 3D rendering and animation, **Form-Z** for modeling, **Adobe After Effects** for compositing and 2D animation and **Commotion** for everything else. Eric has provided a list of several digital effects companies that offer internship programs, along with a list of colleges that provide courses in computer and traditional animation and computer graphics. He also lists some books that cover the principles and methods of visual effects. You can find this information in the appendix at the end of this book.

How does someone get a job in the visual effects field? According to Eric, most effects companies are looking for only two things: experience and a great demo reel. Your reel is made up of shots that you have either done on your own or contributed to in a meaningful way. This is how you show a prospective employer your skills and areas of expertise. It is not mandatory that you go to college, but it is important that you are eager, dedicated and have a talent for this type of work. You also do not need a degree in art, but having a fundamental background in art is very important. Remember, it is always easier to teach an artist to use a computer than to teach a computer-savvy person to be an artist. Check out the website for BlackPool Studios at **www.blackpoolstudios.com**.

SECTION 19

DvGARAGE

DvGarage is a company dedicated to training the next generation of visual media artists around the world. They are providing high quality software and easy to understand training materials to help in the creation of amazing special effects; and they are doing this at a very inexpensive price. Do you want to work with 3D models, lighting or textures? Do you want to work with software that allows for high-quality keying and "blue screen" removal? **DvGarage** offers everything you will need to get started and much more.

DvGarage was started by Alex Lindsay in April of 2000. Building his first 3D model almost 15 years ago, Alex has worked in nearly every area of the industry including programming, print, interactive, real-time 3D, forensics, broadcast, pre-visualization and feature film. His projects have included modeling and animation for the *ABC Hockey Night Open*, crystal development and animation for **Titan AE**, pre-visualization at **JAK Films** and final shots for *Star Wars: Episode 1* at **Industrial Light & Magic**.

Alex has also established himself as an educator working with students from California to Africa. He has been a featured columnist in *3D World, DV Web/Video, 3D Artist, POST*, and others. He has also taught visual effects at San Francisco State University — Multimedia Studies Program.

"It's payback time," says Lindsay, "for every person who gave me a break, a good word, and the advice I needed to succeed in this industry." Alex's co-executive of **DvGarage** is Christopher Marler. Christopher was the director of technology programs at San Francisco State University's College of Extended Learning before he joined **DvGarage**. He was also the director of San Francisco State University's Multimedia Studies program.

DvGarage develops and markets tools and training for both the seasoned visual effects professional and people seeking to enter the field. For beginners, **DvGarage** has the **3D Toolkit**, which includes a true production-level 3D application (a scaled-down version of **Electric Image Universe**), along with 28 step by step tutorials and four hours of video training. It's a great way for people to get started with 3D and to do professional quality modeling and animation.

There is also the **Composite Toolkit**, which is one of the most comprehensive training products for Blue/Green Screen Keying ever created. Not only do you learn real-world solutions to this mysterious art, but you also learn the underlying concepts that make it all work.

DvGarage also offers **DvMatte Pro**. If you are using Mini-DV for industrial, broadband, DVD, games or film work, then **DvMatte Pro** is the fastest, most effective and least expensive professional keyer in the market.

DvGarage also offers more than a dozen other products, covering things like "specialized textures for advanced users" to "tutorial packages for camera mappings." To get a complete list of products and pricing, please visit their website at **www.dvgarage.com**.

We asked **DvGarage** if they had any advice on how to "break in" to the special effects industry. Here's what they said: "Practical experience is everything in the visual effects industry. The demo reel is your calling card, and to really get your foot in the door, you have to have one or more areas of true specialization."

To get your career started, check out **www.dvgarage.com**.

HOW TO START
YOUR OWN
HOME STUDIO

SECTION 20

THE DIGITAL REVOLUTION

What is the digital revolution? With advances in technology happening at such a fast pace, the tools that were once only available to the big studios are now available to anyone. The software that is used to create Hollywood's biggest special effects can now be used on your home computer. The quality of the newest digital cameras is amazing, and even commercial versions of HD (High Definition) cameras are finally being offered to the masses.

The digital revolution has created the opportunity for anyone to jump into the world of filmmaking. In fact, this new technology has allowed people all over the world to work on big Hollywood films from the comfort of their homes. You no longer have to live near Hollywood; the world has been opened to you.

We are living in exciting times...

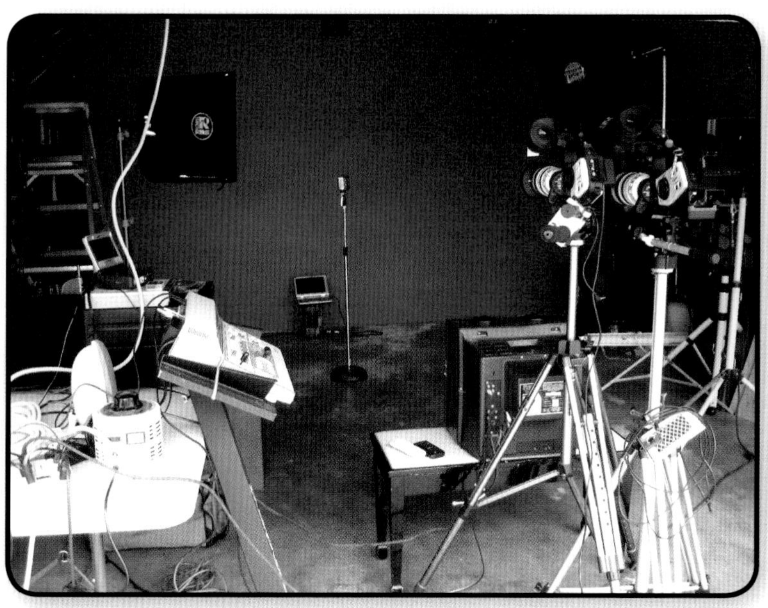

SECTION 21

EQUIPMENT

The number of different products available is staggering, so we will concentrate on the core ingredients of any good home studio. Depending on what services you are going to offer your clients, you might not need all of the equipment that we list; but we will cover all of the basics.

THE COMPUTER

The computer is the centerpiece of your home studio. This is where most of your work will be done. There is a big debate among filmmakers as to which platform is better, **Apple** or **PC**. The answer to this is simple: whichever one best meets your needs. They both have distinct advantages and disadvantages. The final decision will usually come down to your personal comfort level and past experience. Both platforms can provide everything you need to be successful. Some software programs such as **Final Cut Pro** are only available for the Apple platform, but most software programs are available for both Apple and PC computers.

When buying a computer for your home studio, here are some guidelines:

- Buy the fastest computer that you can afford.
- Get as much **RAM** (Random Access Memory) as possible. The absolute minimum you should consider is 1GB (one gigabyte), but get as much as you can.

- Get as much HD (hard drive) space as possible. You will want at least 250GB (250 gigabytes), but get as much as you can. Video files take up a lot of room, and you will fill up your hard drives quickly. If you can afford it, get 500GB or more. If you are planning to work with High Definition footage, you will need to double or triple that amount.

- Consider how you are going to get the video footage into your computer. Does the computer have a Firewire port? Are you going to buy a third-party capture card? Does your computer have an available slot for a third-party capture card? These are all questions you will want to ask yourself and the computer salesman, to make sure your new computer will do everything you expect it to.

- If you are going to buy a third-party capture card, make sure that the computer you buy meets all of the **system requirements** needed by the capture card.

- If you already know what software programs you will be using, make sure your new computer also meets the **system requirements** needed by the software.

- Make your home studio computer a "dedicated" machine if you can. This means that you only run software on this computer that is used for your home studio business. No games, screensavers, school or family programs, etc. Every program that you load can clog your system, make it run slower, and potentially make it crash. The more you can use this computer only for your home studio, the better. Also, it can be a real advantage if you can disconnect this computer from the internet or computer network, and leave it as a stand-alone machine. This will help your computer to work much more efficiently, and help eliminate problems caused by viruses and spyware.

SOFTWARE

Software is your digital toolbox. It provides the tools you need to manipulate your footage in just about any way imaginable. Software tools can help in the following areas of filmmaking:

- Editing
- Compositing
- Painting
- Titling
- 3D modeling and creation
- Sound creation and mixing
- Music creation and mixing
- Color correction
- Film look
- Special Effects
- DVD authoring
- and much more...

Please see the section in this book titled **Digital Software** for more information. There is one area regarding software that most people don't usually think about: **training**. To really get the most out of your software, you should invest in some quality training. This can include anything from a good book, to a class at the local community college, to a training DVD from **www.totaltraining.com**.

THE CAMERA

If you are going to be creating original video content, then the camera is extremely important. The digital revolution has brought some amazing technologies to this field. It seems that the cameras keep improving in quality, with more features, smaller size and a cheaper price. This is great news for the independent or beginning filmmaker. When picking out a camera, there are several factors that you want to consider:

- **Price**: Does it fit within your budget?
- **Features**: Does it do what you need it to do?
- **Digital vs. Analog**: In my opinion, digital cameras are the only way to go. The picture quality of a digital camera is so much better than that of an analog camera. Also, when copying a tape or transferring footage into a computer from an analog camera, you lose quality. Every generation of an analog tape loses quality. Digital cameras do not have this problem. They do not lose quality from copying a tape or transferring footage into a computer. Every generation of a digital tape is exactly the same.
- **How many CCDs does your camera have**? A CCD is a microchip that records the image into the camera. If your camera has three CCDs, also called a 3-chip camera, it has a different microchip for each color (red, green and blue). This results in a much better image. You will definitely want to purchase a 3-chip camera.
- **Standard Definition vs. High Definition**: Eventually you will have to work in High Definition if you want your business to stay competitive. But for now, you can work in either format. Basically, High Definition records more lines of resolution than Standard Definition, and this creates a higher quality picture with more colors and detail. If you decide to shoot and work with HD, make sure your editing software can support HD resolution, and that your computer has the correct inputs to connect to your HD camera.
- **Tape vs. Tapeless**: Most cameras still record to tape. The big problem with tape is that you still have to "capture" the footage into your computer, which can take a lot of time. There are some tapeless solutions available which include recording to **Memory Sticks** or to portable hard drives. One of the advantages of a tapeless system is that you can "copy" the footage onto your computer, which is much faster than "capturing" it. I believe that as new tapeless solutions are unveiled, we will see the death of tape.

- **Filters and adapters**: If your camera does not shoot in widescreen format, you might need to buy a wide-angle adapter for your camera. Also, there are a multitude of other filters, matte boxes and adapters available. Please check out **www.schneideroptics.com** for a sampling. When picking a camera, make sure there are filters and adapters available for it.
- Which companies make the best cameras for independent and beginning filmmakers?
    - **Sony (www.sonystyle.com)**
    - **Panasonic (www.panasonic.com)**
    - **Canon (www.canon.com)**
    - **JVC (www.jvc.com)**

CAMERA SUPPORT

Camera support is very important. Unless you want your entire movie to look like *The Blair Witch Project*, you will need something to stabilize your camera. The most common type of camera support is the **Tripod**. To get an idea of what is available, check out the following sites:

- **www.bhphotovideo.com**
- **www.amvona.com**.

The tripod is used to keep the camera stationary and perfectly still.

Movement of the camera is important for certain types of shots. You can change how a shot "feels" by adding a little movement to the camera. But how do you move the camera without making the audience get motion sickness? Three of the most common ways include a **camera stabilizer** device, a **dolly** or a **crane**. To get an idea of what types of camera stabilizer devices are available, check out the following sites:

- **www.varizoom.com**
- **www.steadicam.com**
- **www.glidecam.com**

To get an idea of what types of dollies are available, check out the following sites:

- **www.microdolly.com**
- **www.glideshot.com**
- **www.indiedolly.com**

To get an idea of what types of cranes are available, check out the following sites:

- **www.nuangle.com**
- **www.ezfx.com**
- **www.glidecam.com**

There are also several sites on the internet that will show you how to build these types of devices very cheaply. These sites can be easily found with an internet search.

SOUND

Sound is 50% of the movie experience. The next time you are watching a movie on DVD, turn off the sound. You will realize how boring the movie is without the dialogue, sound effects and music. Please see the sections in this book titled **Digital Software** and **A Word about Sound Effects** for more information about sound software, sound effects and music.

What does the independent or beginning filmmaker need to record great sound for his movies? The first thing you need is a high-quality microphone. This can be a shotgun microphone, a wireless microphone or a combination of both. If you are serious about your home studio business, the microphone that comes attached to your camera is not going to cut it. To get an idea of what types of microphones are available, check out the following sites:

- **www.sennheiserusa.com**
- **www.audio-technica.com**
- **www.azdencorp.com**

Just as a side note, if your budget can afford it, the **Sennheiser K6-ME66** is an excellent microphone with great sound quality.

How will you connect the microphone to your camera? Most **consumer** cameras and microphones use a 1/8" stereo or mono connector. Most **professional** cameras and microphones use an XLR connector. What do you do if your camera has a 1/8" stereo connector and your microphone has an XLR connector? This is actually a common scenario among beginning filmmakers. The answer is an **XLR Adapter Box**. This box will allow you to connect your XLR microphone to your cameras 1/8" stereo connector. To get an idea of what types of XLR adapter boxes are available, check out the following sites:

- **www.beachtek.com**
- **www.studio1productions.com**
- **www.signvideo.com**

How will you mount your microphone? You will need to buy a **boom pole**, **shock mount** and **windscreen**. The boom pole is a long pole that can have a shock mount attached to one end. The shock mount holds your microphone and helps to eliminate boom handling noise. The windscreen is a cover for your microphone which helps to reduce noise caused by the wind. To get an idea of what types of boom poles, shock mounts and windscreens are available, check out the following sites:

- **www.bhphotovideo.com**
- **www.locationsound.com**
- **www.coffeysound.com**

There are also several sites on the internet that will show you how to build these types of devices very cheaply. These sites can be easily found with an internet search.

LIGHTING

Lighting is a very important part of your productions. It is one of the main tools you have for changing the look and feel of your shots. Lighting can set the mood and dramatically increase the quality of your production. This book does not have the space to teach you proper lighting techniques, but I wanted to mention it because it is extremely important and needs to be a consideration in your home studio business. I would highly recommend that you seek out good training materials, such as books, training DVDs or lighting classes. To get an idea of what types of lights are available, check out the following internet sites:

- **www.bhphotovideo.com**
- **www.lowel.com**
- **www.imagewest.tv**
- **www.jtlcorp.com**

The downside to lighting is that it can take a lot of time and cost extra money that you might not have. If you can't afford lighting equipment, you will at least want to purchase a **Reflector**. They come in all different shapes and sizes, but are usually circle-shaped with a reflective coating on one side. If there are any available light sources, you can use the reflector to redirect that light to where you want it. This is especially useful when you are shooting outside and can use the sun as a light source.

SECTION 22

THE BUSINESS

When starting your own home studio, the internet can be your best friend. I know this might sound a little unbelievable, but the internet can literally open up your business to the world. We live in unprecedented times, and the home studio owner needs every advantage he can get.

COMPANY IMAGE

Image is everything. There is an old saying, "It's not *what* you know, it's *who* you know." This saying is very true. If you are fortunate enough to already have some contacts in the filmmaking world, you are way ahead of the game. However, if you are like most people and haven't developed those connections yet, then your image is everything; and you need to put a lot of time and effort into creating it.

When you are first starting out, most companies and filmmaking professionals will not want to talk to you. They will look for any excuse to dismiss you, as they try to sift through the many letters and calls that they receive from people just like you. Most companies will not give you a chance, so you need to make sure you are ready when one of them does. You don't want people to view your business as a small home studio; you want them to perceive you as a big professional studio that is successful and experienced. How do you create that image?

- **Business name and logo**: Your business name and logo speak volumes about you and your studio. Different markets expect different things. Are you trying to cater to the local community or are you trying to make it in Hollywood? If your market is the local community, then you can get by with a funny or "cutesy" name and logo. If you are trying to break into Hollywood, then your name must be adept, eliciting thoughts of professionalism and experience. No one will take you seriously if you don't. The same is true for your logo. You want people to remember your name and logo once they see them, but not because they were obnoxious or corny. If you are not talented in graphic design yourself, you may want to hire a professional to help create your business name and logo. They are more important than you might realize.

- **Website and email address**: When someone is considering working with you, they will usually check your website first. Consequently, this will probably be their first impression of you. This could make or break the deal before you even get a chance to talk with them. Your website is your calling card to the world. If you don't have a great website, then people will probably think you don't have a great studio. You have just given them a reason to dismiss you. Your website is a reflection of your business, so treat it that way. If you are not skilled in web design, then hire a professional to design and implement your site. As for your email address, make sure that whoever provides your website for you also includes an email address with the same domain name. For example, let's say you sign-up with **Yahoo.com** to host your website. Your business name is **Studio 11**, so you get a website with the domain name of **www.studio11.com**. Make sure they include an email address as part of the package, so your email address will be **michael@studio11.com** instead of **michael@yahoo.com** or **michael@google.com**. Most people will associate an address that ends in **@google.com** or **@yahoo.com** as someone who is working out of their home. Most people will associate an address ending in **@studio11.com** as someone working at a big studio. Who do you think they are going to pursue? Not everyone will have these types of associations, but are you willing to take a chance?
- **Printing**: The four things you must have are professional business cards, letterhead, envelopes and access to a good printer. Whenever

you are corresponding with people through the mail, they will judge you and your studio by the quality of your "presentation"; make sure your printing is high quality and professional. Remember, people are looking for any reason to dismiss you, so don't give them one. Always send typed letters on your high -quality letterhead. When you are sending any type of correspondence through the mail, always include your business card paper-clipped to the top of your letter. If you are sending a letter that requires a response, always include a self-addressed stamped envelope. Never try to impress people by drawing or coloring on the outside of the envelope. This will guarantee that your letter ends up in the trash.

- **Business phone and fax**: It is mandatory that you have a dedicated phone line for your home studio. You must also have an answering machine with a very professional-sounding message. Anyone who calls you will expect nothing less. In addition, a lot of people still use fax machines to conduct business. If you don't have one, this will affect your image, and may give them a reason to dismiss you. People in this industry can be very fickle.
- **Business license and checking account**: You will want to get a business license for your studio. After that, you will need to setup a business checking account with a local bank. Once you start getting paying clients, they will pay you by check, and will make them payable to your business name. You will need the business checking account to cash these checks. I know this is common sense, but it's important to cover the basics.

LEGAL PROTECTION

How do you protect your studio and your work? Let's be honest, not everyone in this world is trustworthy. Some people will sue you every chance they get and others will steal your work to sell off as their own. How can a home studio owner protect himself?

- **Insurance**: Insurance can be expensive, but it can also save your business. Make sure you have plenty of insurance to cover your equipment and plenty of liability insurance to protect yourself. Most places won't let you film at their locations unless you have liability insurance. They want to make sure everything will be covered if you break something or if someone gets hurt.

- **Contracts**: Any business agreements you make with someone else should include a signed contract. It doesn't matter how big or small the agreement is, you need a signed contract. There are several sites on the internet that will provide sample contracts for you to use. These can be found with an internet search.

- **Releases**: Whenever you are working with actors, crew members or locations, you should always get a signed release. Basically, the release should give you permission to film them and then to use those images for whatever purposes you deem necessary. It should also release you from any type of liability if something bad were to happen. Lastly, it should include any monetary agreements you have made. These are just guidelines, not legal advice. There are several sites on the internet that provide sample release forms for you to use; these can be found with an internet search. If you have any questions or concerns, you should consult an attorney.

- **WGA (Writers Guild of America)**: If you are trying to protect your work such as a script, book, treatment, etc., you can register it with the WGA. Just browse to their website at **www.wgaregistry.org**, and for $20 anyone can register their work with them.

- **Copyright**: In addition to the WGA, you may want to send a copy of your work to the Library of Congress. Their website is **www.copyright.gov**. For $45, you can get your work copyrighted.

- **Poor Man's Protection**: At the very least, you should mail yourself a copy of your work, and make sure you don't open the envelope once you get it back from the post office. This will be a sealed document that is date stamped by the post office. This is not as good as the WGA or getting a copyright, but it is better than nothing.

NETWORKING

To really make it in this business, you need to develop relationships with other people that are also in this business. You will want to make as many connections as you can. Create a list of all the people you interact with including their name, company, email address and phone number. This list will grow longer over time, and can be a valuable resource when you are in need. You never know when someone you met three years ago might be just the person you need to help you now. Once you build a network of people, you will have a strong base of resources from which to draw. Just remember to help others as much as you can, and they will be there to help you when the need arises.

SECTION 23

LESSONS LEARNED

What does it take to be successful? It takes a lot of time, a lot of work and a lot of dedication. This business can take up more time than you probably realize, but the rewards can be amazing. Be careful not to neglect your family and friends; they are part of what makes life so magical. If you decide to partner with someone, make sure they share your passion and dedication. It is tough to have your dreams fall apart because your partner is not willing to do their share. I know this is all common sense, but sometimes we just need a little reminder from someone who's been there.

LOCATIONS

When you are filming your first movie, you may be inspired to include a lot of different locations. For your first effort, remember that less is more. Try to use as few locations as possible. The fewer the locations you have, the easier and quicker you can complete your movie. Once you have decided how many locations you will need, keep the following thoughts in mind:

- You can usually get your locations for free if you just ask around. Most people love the idea of having their business, office or property in a movie. If you need a restaurant, ask around at all the local restaurants. Let them know that you can't afford to pay them, but that you will give them credit in the movie, and that it will be free publicity for them. If they say no, just move on to the next one. I have always found locations for my movies this way.

- Some people might require you to have liability insurance. If you don't have insurance, just keep asking around until you find someone that doesn't require insurance. If you find a place that you just have to film at, and they require insurance, some insurance companies offer one-day event insurance. You will just have to check with several insurance companies until you find one that offers this type of insurance.

CASTING

Once you have your script done, where do you find the actors to bring your vision to life? One option is to cast your friends. The good news is that they will probably work for free; the bad news is that they may have no acting ability whatsoever. So how do you find talented and experienced actors that will work for free? Here are two options:

- **Colleges and universities**: Call and talk with the drama department at your local colleges and universities. They will usually post an ad for you on their bulletin board. Just include a short sentence about the movie, what parts you are casting for, a contact phone number, and the date, time and location of the casting call.

- **Back Stage**: **Back Stage** is a national casting resource that features print and online editions. It reaches over 150,000 experienced performers every month. Back Stage can be reached at (323) 525-2358, and their website is **www.backstage.com**. Once you register with Back Stage (which is free), you can post your casting notice, which will appear both online and in their print edition. There may be a small charge to post the casting notice, so please check with Back Stage for more information. When posting your notice, you will be asked to provide some information about yourself and your movie. Here is some advice:

    - Advertise as non-union (unless you are union)
    - Ask for a picture and resume
    - Specify that it is not for money, but for food and credit

  - DO NOT give a phone number or street address
  - Give a PO box address for all correspondence (if you don't have a PO box, get one)

- Once you advertise in **Back Stage**, you will receive a lot of headshots and resumes. Don't be surprised if you receive several hundred; this is not an exaggeration. The reason that you don't want to give a phone number or street address is for your own safety and convenience. You never know what an actor might do to secure a role in your next movie. Don't give them an opportunity to invade your home or privacy. Also, you probably don't want to receive hundreds of phone calls on your home studio phone. Once you have gone through all the resumes, pick the best three or four actors for each part, and invite them to the casting call. You need to contact every person that sent you a resume, even if you aren't considering them for a part. You will want to thank them for their interest, but inform them you have picked someone else. This can be very time consuming, but it is expected and needs to be done.

- You might want to send a scripted scene to each of the actors that you are considering. This way they will come to the casting call prepared.

FILM COMMISSIONS

A film commission is usually a local team of professionals that can help you with your filmmaking needs. They can support you in many ways including the following:

- Preliminary scouting of potential sites, including photographs

- Provide information on locations, weather, crew, services and suppliers

- Serve as liaison between local, state, and federal agencies and the private sector

- Assist in securing permits and clearances

Most film commissions will provide these services for free, but contact your local commission for any possible fees.

How do you find your local film commission? One way is to check on the site **www.filmcommissionhq.com**. They might be able to help you track down your local film commission.

ADDITIONAL RESOURCES

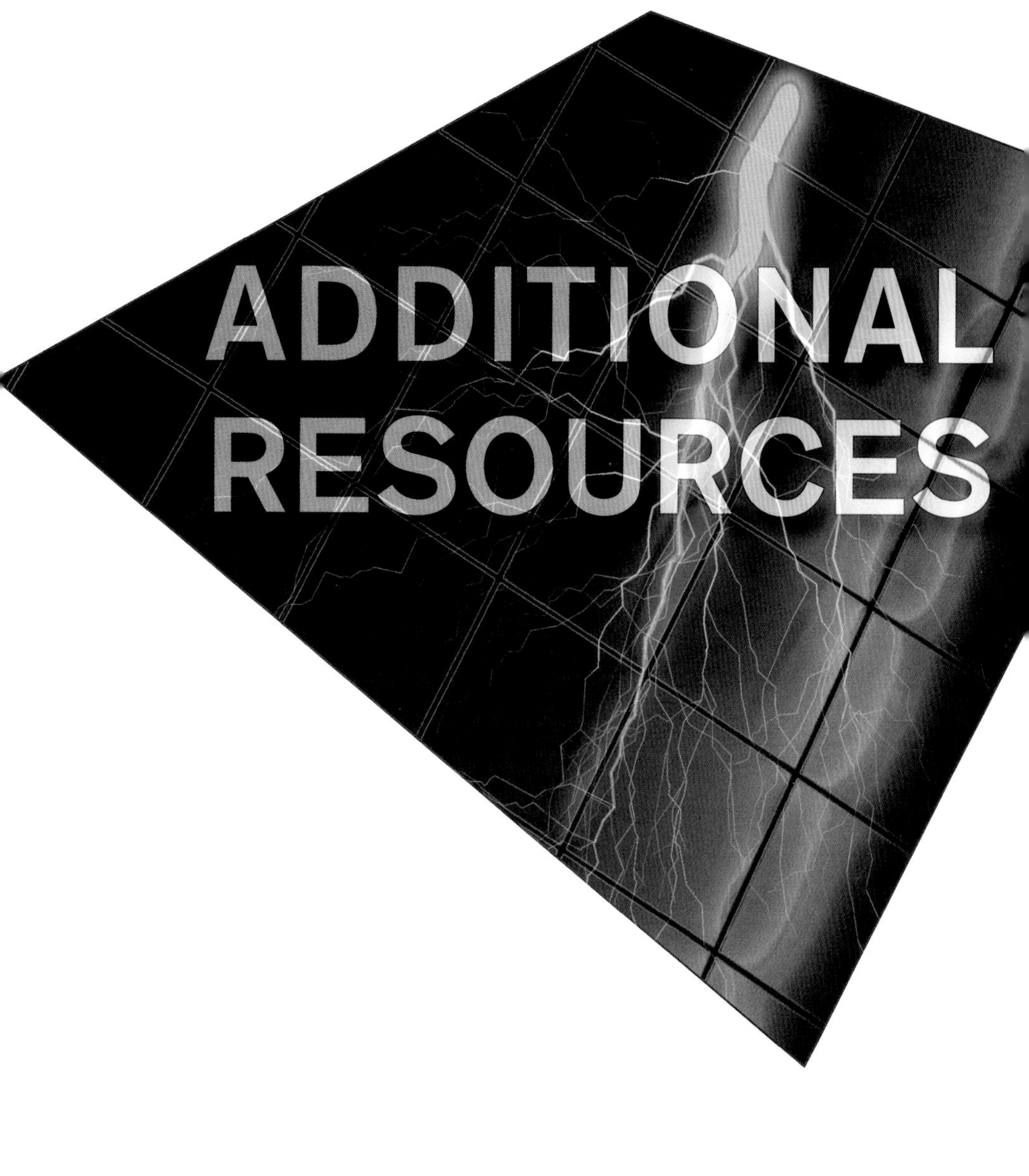

SECTION 24

THE MASTER COURSE IN BLOCKING AND STAGING

Besides working with actors, **blocking** and **camera work** are two of the most important jobs a director does. (Blocking is the movement and positioning of the actors in a shot. Camera work is the movement and positioning of the cameras to capture the shot.) Unfortunately, most books, videos and many film schools barely touch the basics.

How can beginning or independent filmmakers learn these valuable skills? One way is with the **Master Course in High-End Blocking and Staging** training course on DVD. It may be the most comprehensive and ambitious directing course in the world.

This course builds a complete understanding of camera work from the ground up, and is intended to be useful for filmmakers on every level.

What will this course teach you?

- Learn feature and network-quality directing
- Become a master of blocking techniques by watching almost a thousand 3D animation examples
- Get a profound understanding of every conceivable camera and actor movement
- Perform more effective and cohesive blocking using fewer setups
- Create more production value for your movies
- Become an expert at using a dolly and crane
- Learn how to block any scene from scratch
- Create complex scenes without line-issues and editing problems
- Finally be able to concentrate on the actors
- Learn how easy it can be to do great camera work

The primary goal of the **Master Course** is to teach you the most effective blocking with the highest production-value and to help you build a vast repertoire of techniques to make directing more expressive — and ultimately more fun.

This course was created by director **Per Holmes,** who has spent over half a decade developing an all-inclusive language of high-end camera work. He started this project for his own personal use, and then realized how much others would benefit from these techniques.

The **Master Course** is made up of six volumes. The first four volumes are all about building a comprehensive language of camera moves that apply equally well to any type of shooting. Volumes one and two deal with stationary camera work and focuses especially on shot selection, framing, managing the line for complex scenes, creating a library of ready-made camera-plots, psychology of character placement/movement, and maximizing the use of depth. Volumes three and four deal exclusively with teaching you hundreds of dolly and crane techniques that will dramatically increase the production-value of your next shoot. Volumes five and six teach a powerful blocking method that produces excellent results for the vast majority of scenes. It also presents many staged scenes that demonstrate how the different techniques can work together.

Basically, this course will teach you how to set up your shots, where to place the cameras, how to use camera movement in your scene and how to pick the angles and moves that best bring out the emotions in the scene.

This course presents all of its techniques as 3D animations that you can watch. When the course is teaching you how to perform a camera move, you actually get to watch how the camera move is done, and then you get to see what the final shot would look like. This approach is very effective in teaching you how and why these techniques are used.

The underlying focus throughout the course is on creating the most elegant shots possible. To get an idea of what the course looks like, please see the following examples:

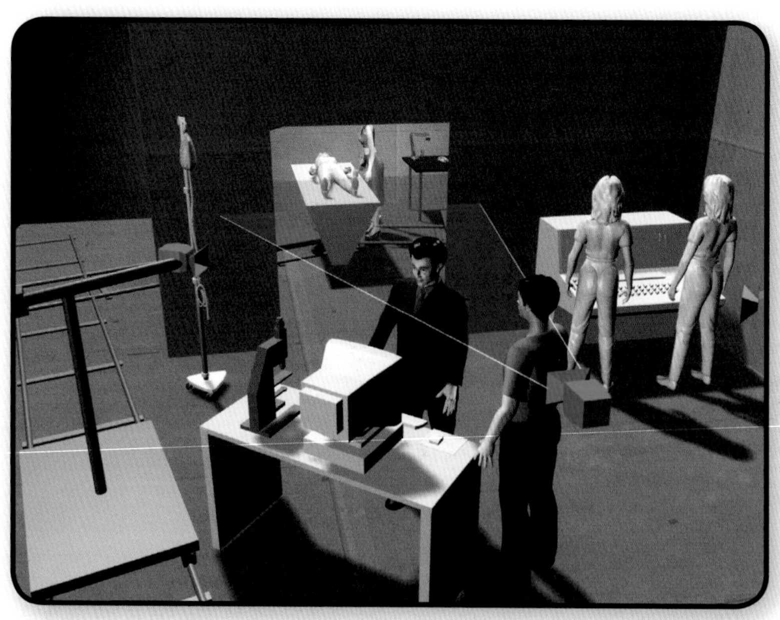

SECTION 25

PIXEL CORPS

Alex Lindsay is the Chief Architect and Founder of the **Pixel Corps**. He started programming graphics on an Apple IIe in 1982 and 15 years later was working on **Star Wars: Episode 1** at **Industrial Light and Magic** as part of the "Rebel Mac Unit."

From the very beginning, Alex searched for **Digital Media** training and resources. He tried schools, books and conferences, and while these were somewhat useful, they never provided the full range of training that Alex was looking for.

After 20 years of frustration at not finding the training and resources he wanted, he decided to create the **Pixel Corps**. The Pixel Corps was designed to provide:

- Clear guidelines for learning digital media
- Inexpensive and ongoing education in the ever-changing business of digital media
- Access to people and equipment that most of us wouldn't otherwise have
- A community of artisans, all dedicated to moving both the technology and each other forward
- Access to true production training and experience

The Pixel Corps currently has over 1500 members in more than 20 countries. There is a small monthly fee to join the Pixel Corps, so please visit their website at **www.pixelcorps.com** for more information. When you become a member, you get access to the following:

VIDEO TRAINING

Members get access to a large and growing library of video training (currently over 90 hours), with new material being added each session. Topics covered in the training include:

- 3D Modeling/Texturing
- Animation
- Photoshop
- Motion Capture
- Compositing
- HDRi
- Matchmoving
- Photogrammetry
- Understanding the Visual FX Pipeline

SOFTWARE

Members receive 3- to 12-month licenses for selected applications. Current applications include:

- 2d3 Boujou
- Apple Shake
- Maxon Cinema 4D
- RealViz Image Modeler
- RealViz Stitcher
- RealViz Matchmover Pro
- Softimage XSI

CHALLENGES

Members are challenged to work on specific projects in the areas of photography, 2D, motion graphics and 3D. As hundreds of members work on the same problem at the same time, the concept of peer-to-peer learning becomes clear. Members will receive a number of challenges each session requiring varying levels of skill. Many of the challenges include source files to start with.

COMMUNITY FORUMS

The **Pixel Corp**s provides closed forums for members to trade ideas and projects, and get input from in-house experts. The growing online community is unlike anything else in the world and it's one of the greatest benefits of membership.

PRODUCTION TRAINING

Members will be eligible to join international teams to produce large projects that are designed to build production skills and reels. Some projects will involve over 50 people and include Motion Capture, HDRi and HD resources.

The industry is changing too fast to get a "degree" and assume it will still be useful a year later. The learning process has to be ongoing, and quality training is now available. Check out the Pixel Corps at **www.pixelcorps.com**.

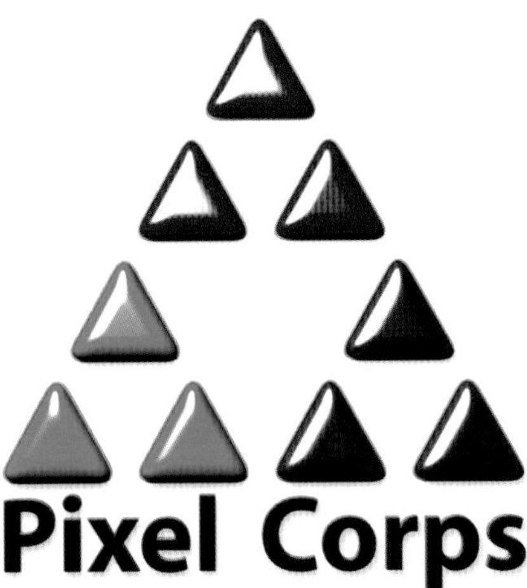

SECTION 26

VIDEO COPILOT

Video Copilot was founded in 2003 by **Andrew Kramer**. It was created as a resource for visual effects artists and talented visionaries seeking all the benefits of a digital postproduction. Andrew has worked as a producer, director, editor, compositor and key grip, so he knows what it's like to be responsible for every aspect of a production. He knows how hard it is to be a filmmaker, so he has created some amazing tutorials that highlight real-world production issues and provide solutions that work.

Video Copilot has created some great products to help visual effects artists and filmmakers. I want to highlight three of their products, but please check out their website at **www.videocopilot.net** for a complete listing of what they have to offer.

ACTION MOVIE ESSENTIALS

Special effects have never been easier than with **Action Movie Essentials**. This CD contains a fantastic collection of 60 stock footage elements for video professionals. These elements include the following effects:

- Muzzle flashes
- Bullet ricochets
- Bullet holes
- Explosions
- Blood spatter
- Blood bursts

- Fog
- Smoke

All of the elements arrive in **QuickTime** format with built-in transparency, so there is no keying or matting required. You can just import these elements into your favorite compositing or editing program, and you are ready to go.

FILM MAGIC PRO

How do you obtain that elusive **film look** for your movie, when your production was not shot with an extremely expensive film camera? One way is with **Film Magic Pro**. Utilizing this product, you can perform the following:

- Create dramatic color grading during video finishing
- Achieve the look of popular movies and commercials
- Enhance the look of digital video
- Improve the look of 3D animations and motion graphics

Film Magic Pro includes the following features:

- 50 unique cinema style presets for **After Effects 6.5 Pro**
- Imitate the look of popular movies, commercials, and music videos
- Execute eight great cinematic transitions
- Enjoy fast rendering times compared to similar packages
- Works with HD, NTSC & PAL footage
- Use on any frame rate: 60i, 50i, 30P, 25P, 24P, 24Pa, etc.
- Includes a step-by-step video tutorial with advanced techniques

This amazing collection of Cinema Styles will transform your everyday video into the feature look of primetime television — all with simplicity never before seen. Easily audition every look until you find the one that complements your creative vision. Utilizing dramatic color correction formulas, Film Magic Pro takes your video beyond the raw and untreated look you've settled for in the past. Simply adjust the input exposure for your video footage and Film Magic Pro will do the rest.

SERIOUS EFFECTS AND COMPOSITING

Most serious visual effects artists will work with **Adobe After Effects** sometime during their career, as this program is the industry standard. This DVD tutorial from **Video Copilot** requires that your computer is DVD-capable, and that you have access to either **Adobe After Effects** version **6.5** or **7**.

Learn how to perform effects major studios pay hundreds of thousands of dollars to create. In this exciting, end-to-end tutorial DVD, you will discover real-world techniques and time-saving procedures not found in the manual. Each video tutorial covers a specific objective from start to finish. This DVD is divided into ten full-length tutorials and includes over three hours of training. The topics covered are:

- Getting started and new features
- Basic color keying
- 3D silhouette
- Cruise control
- Advanced muzzle fire
- Blown away (explosion)
- Floating text
- DVD menu creation I & II
- The teleporter
- Selective color creation

If you want to take your visual effects skills to the next level, this training is for you. Please see the examples on the following pages for a sampling of what you will learn:

ADDITIONAL WEB PAGES TO CHECK OUT:

www.ilm.com/theshow
This page explores some of the special effects from the Disney movie *Pirates of the Caribbean: Dead Man's Chest*

www.webfilmschool.com
Hollywood Film Institute
Dov S-S Simens' "2-Day Film School," "DVD Film School," "Streaming Film School" and Hollywood Bookstore

www.filmmaking.net
Great resource for independent filmmakers

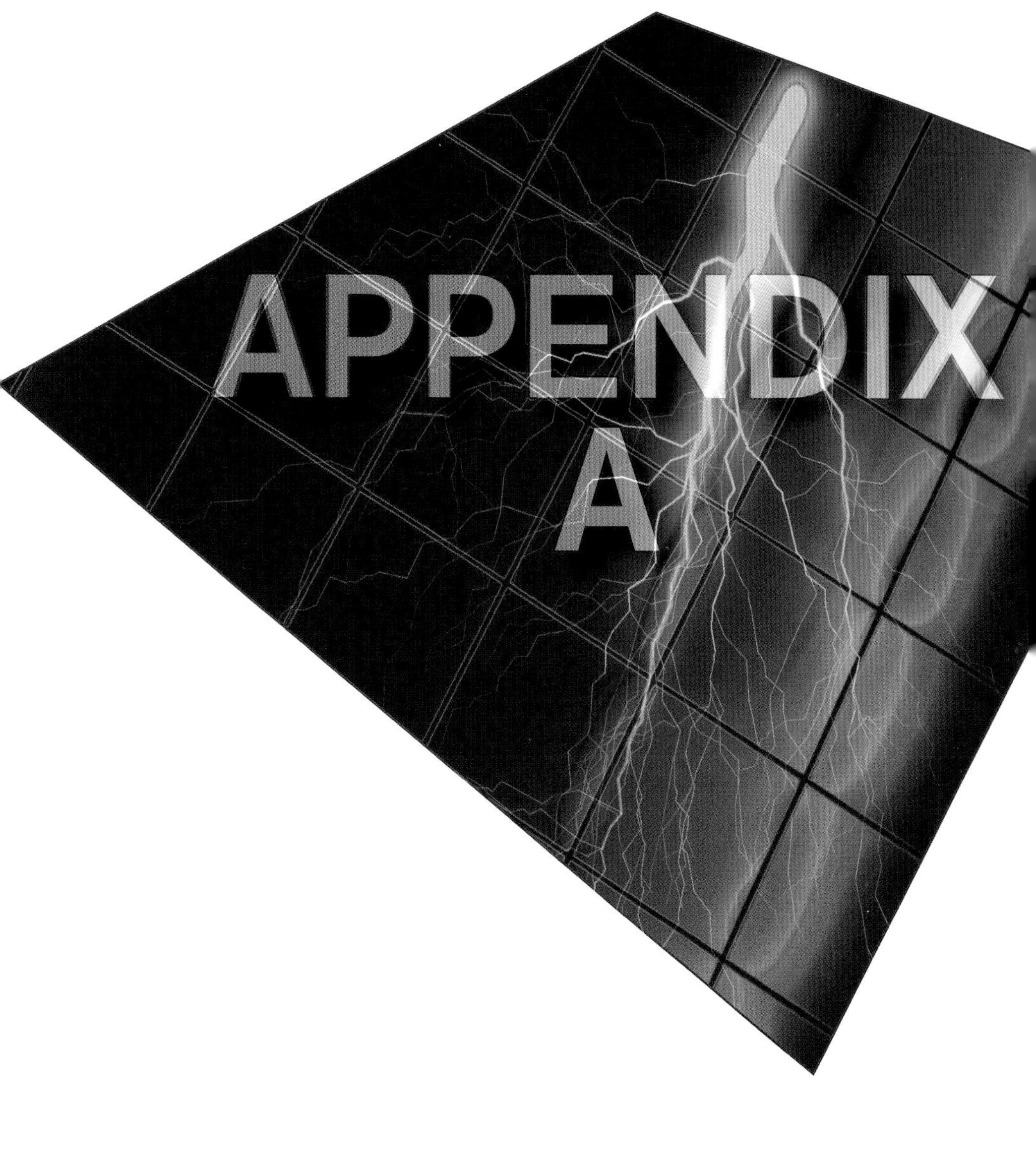
APPENDIX
A

SECTION 27

A WORD ABOUT SOUND EFFECTS

Most people might not realize the importance of sound. It does not matter how realistic your gun flashes look; the effect won't be believable or complete without the accompanying sound of the gunshot. Imagine a shot of someone getting punched. It does not matter how well the actors execute their moves; the scene is not exciting or complete until you hear the "meaty thud" of the punch. The sound makes the effect believable and much more exciting. Sounds for digital editing systems usually come in two formats, **wav** and **mp3**. There are many places to get quality sound effects and some of them are free.

You can download **wav** files and **mp3** files from many sites on the Internet. Just do a search on "free wav files" or something similar. Also, check out sites like **www.soundamerica.com** and **www.wavcentral.com** as well.

You can also buy professional sound effects from companies like **The Hollywood Edge** (**www.hollywoodedge.com**) and **Sound Ideas** (**www.sound-ideas.com.**) Sound Ideas also sells collections of sounds from **Lucasfilm** and **Universal Studios**, among others.

If you still cannot find what you are looking for, you can always try creating the sounds yourself. This can be a lot of fun, and also very educational. The next time you watch a movie, try to concentrate on the sound effects. This can be a great place to learn what sound is all about.

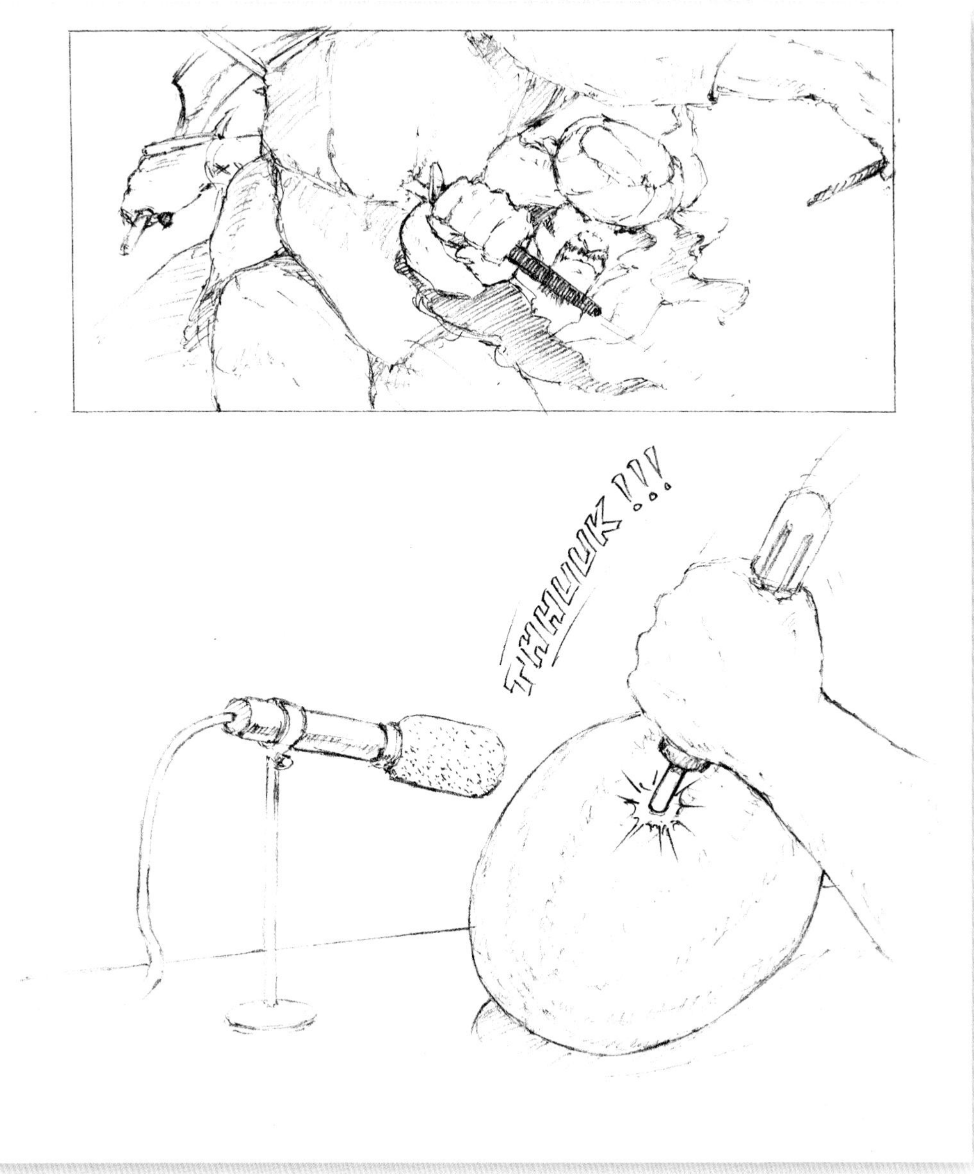
THHUUK!!!

SOUND EFFECTS COMPANIES

Sound effects companies sell every type of sound imaginable. You can find everything from airplanes to alien spaceships. Good sound effects can truly take your movie to the next level. Here are some companies that offer quality sound effects.

The Hollywood Edge
www.hollywoodedge.com
(800) 292-3755

Sound Ideas
www.sound-ideas.com
(905) 886-5000

Studio Cutz
www.studiocutz.com
(866) 252-7788

Futurity
www.futurityfx.com
(408) 354-4432

Sound Effects
www.soundeffects.com
(888) 826-5855

SECTION 28

STORYBOARDS

Storyboards can help you visualize how a scene will look. It allows you to plan out your shots before actually filming anything. This gives you the creative freedom to experiment with different shots until you come up with the perfect scene. This is especially useful for complex or special effects sequences. Sometimes a movie only uses storyboards for difficult sequences, while other times the entire movie is storyboarded. It allows you to work faster on the movie set, and it also gives the actors an idea of what they are going to be shooting.

Please see the storyboard examples on the following pages. When creating your storyboards, you do not have to be a talented artist. You can use stick figures or simple shapes. This is just to help you visualize the different shots you will need to complete your sequence.

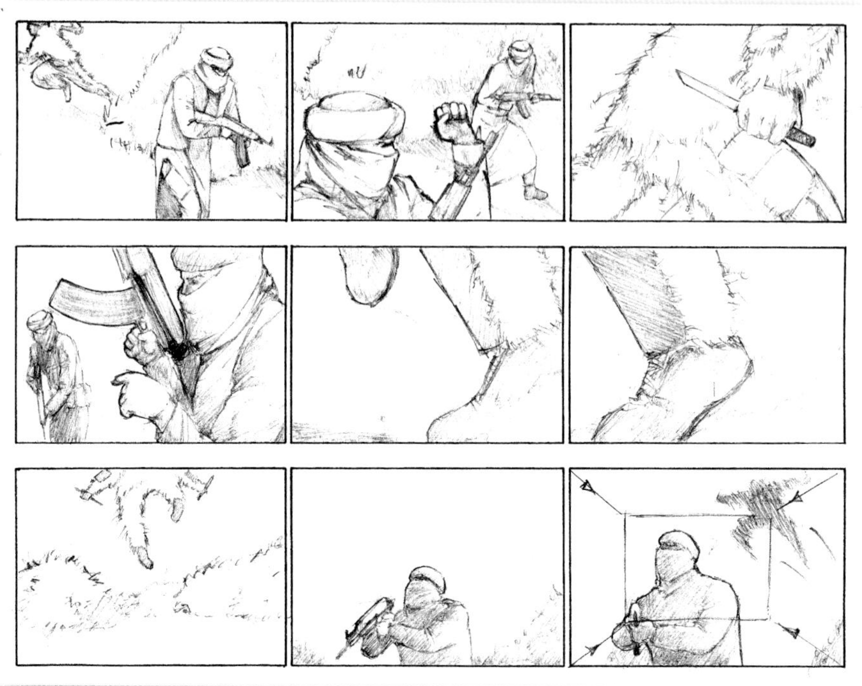

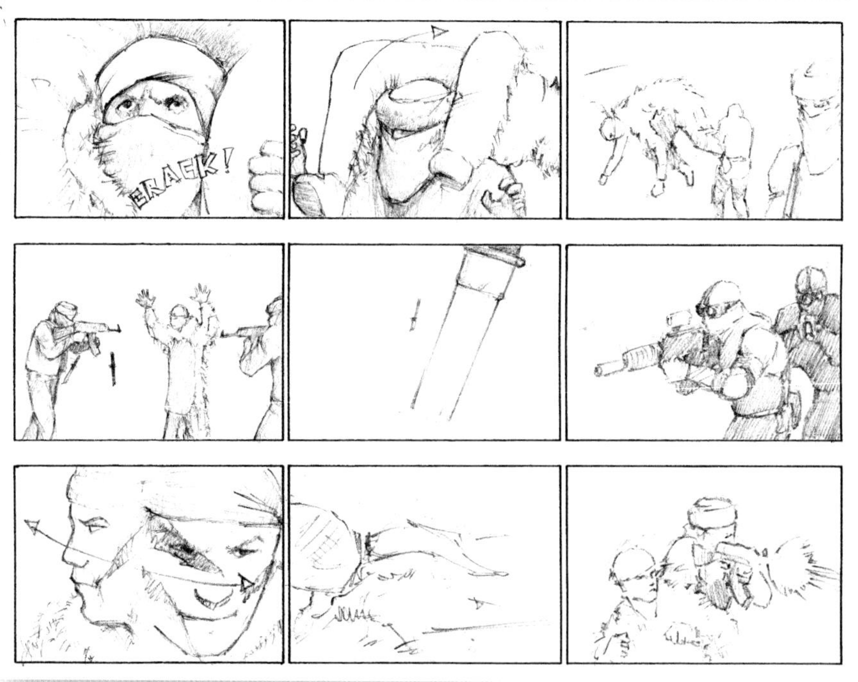
CRACK!

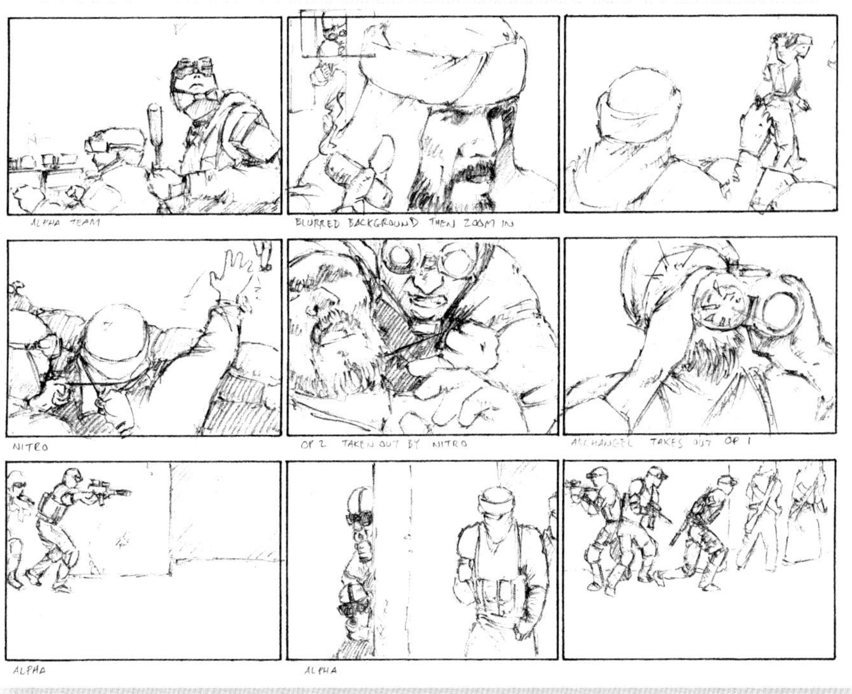
ALPHA TEAM
BLURRED BACKGROUND THEN ZOOM IN
NITRO
OP 2 TAKEN OUT BY NITRO
ARCHANGEL TAKES OUT OP 1
ALPHA
ALPHA

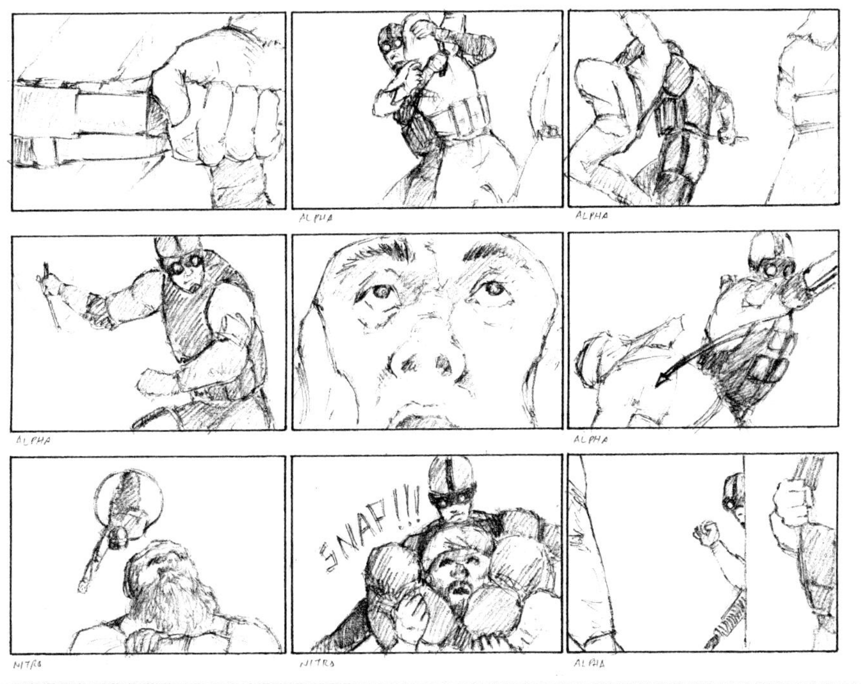
ALPHA
ALPHA
ALPHA
ALPHA
NITRO
SNAP!!!
NITRO
ALPHA

SECTION 29

DVD SPECIAL FEATURES

Some DVDs have special features included on the disc. Special features can include behind-the-scenes documentaries, cast and crew interviews, director commentary, segments on visual effects and a host of other information. These special features are a valuable resource for the low-budget or beginning filmmaker. They can teach you about the different aspects of filmmaking, including special effects. The DVDs listed below include some excellent special feature sections. This is not a complete list.

The Lord of the Rings: The Fellowship of the Ring **Special Extended Edition**
New Line Home Entertainment

The Lord of the Rings: The Two Towers **Special Extended Edition**
New Line Home Entertainment

The Lord of the Rings: The Return of the King **Special Extended Edition**
New Line Home Entertainment

The Matrix
Warner Bros.

The Matrix Revisited
Warner Bros.

The Bourne Identity **Extended Edition**
Universal Pictures

Coronado
Fireworks Pictures

Gladiator
DreamWorks Home Entertainment

***Indiana Jones* Bonus Material**
Lucasfilm Ltd.

***Spider-Man 2* Special Edition**
Sony Pictures Home Entertainment

***Armageddon*: The Criterion Collection**
Touchstone Home Video

***Terminator 2: Judgment Day* Ultimate Edition**
Artisan Home Entertainment

Once Upon a Time in Mexico
Colombia Pictures

M:I-2
Paramount Pictures

SECTION 30

FAN FILMS

What is a Fan Film? **Wikipedia (**http://www.wikipedia.org**)** defines it as: **"**A **fan film** is a film or video inspired by a movie, television show, comic book or a similar source, created by fans rather than by the source's copyright holders or creators. Fan filmmakers have traditionally been amateurs, but some of the more notable films have actually been produced by professional filmmakers as film school class projects or as demonstration reels. Fan films vary tremendously in length, from short faux-teaser trailers for non-existent motion pictures to rarer full-length motion pictures."

Basically, a Fan Film is a way for you to showcase your filmmaking talents. They can be a lot of fun and a great outlet for your creativity. Check out the websites below for examples of what a Fan Film is.

http://www.theforce.net/fanfilms

http://www.fanfilms.net

http://www.atomfilms.com/af/spotlight/collections/starwars

http://www.batmanfanfilms.com

http://www.ifilm.com/?sctn=fanfilms&pg=fanfilms&htv=12

http://www.swfanfilms.com

http://www.panicstruckpro.com/revelations

http://www.theonering.net/fanfilms

http://www.theraider.net/community/theater/index.php

http://www.collorastudios.com/projects/bde/bdemain.htm

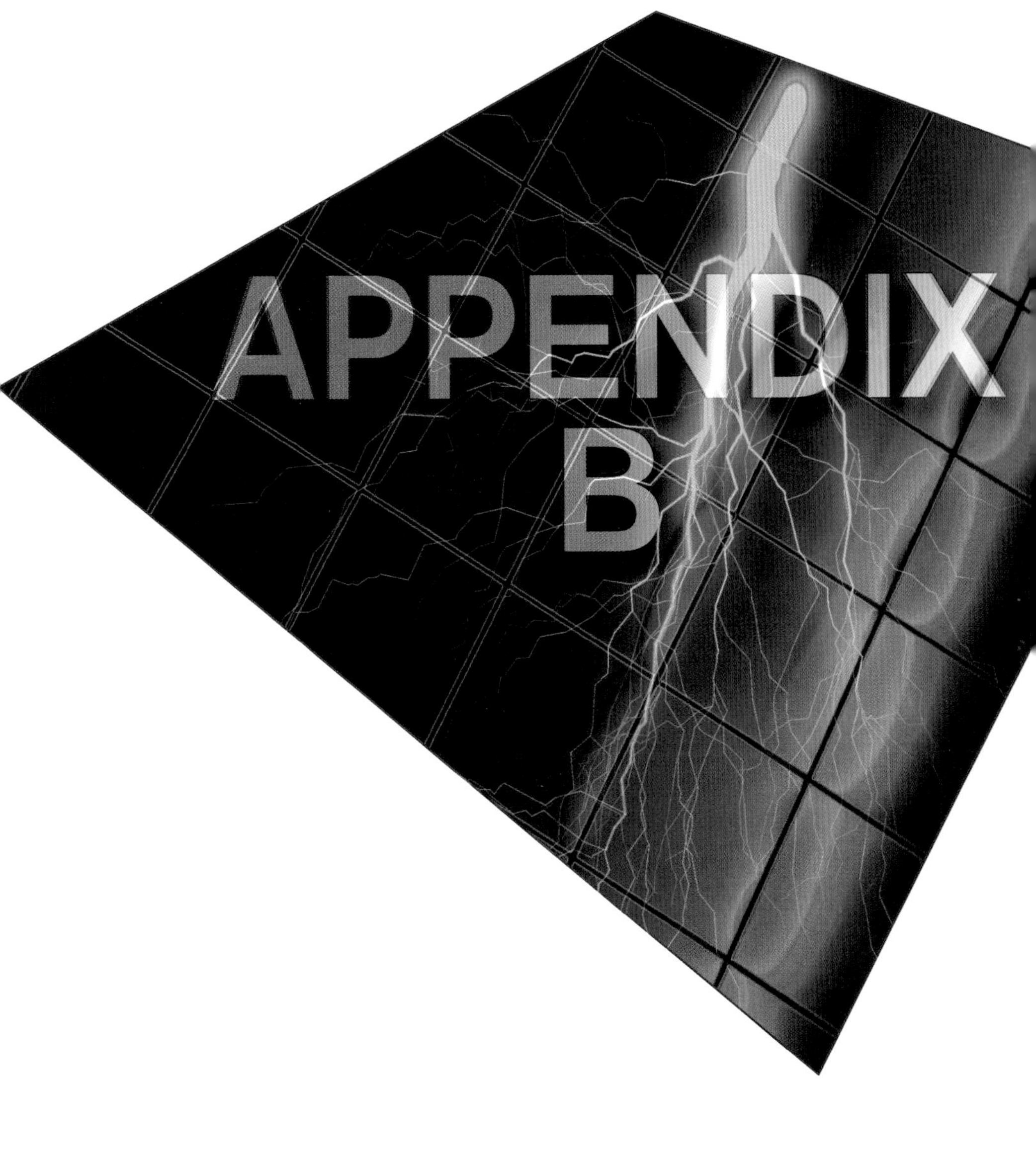
APPENDIX
B

SECTION 31

DIGITAL EFFECTS COMPANIES THAT OFFER INTERNSHIPS

(INFORMATION PROVIDED BY BLACKPOOL STUDIOS)

Industrial Light & Magic
http://www.ilm.com/internship.html

Sony Imageworks
http://www.imageworks.com/career.html

Digital Domain
http://www.digitaldomain.com (click on careers, then internships)

PDI\ Dreamworks
http://www.dreamworksanimation.com/dwa/opencms/careers/dreamworks_pdi/internships.jsp

Rhythm and Hues
http://www.rhythm.com/inside_randh/opportunities_internships.shtml

Matte World Digital
http://www.matteworld.com/hr/

SECTION 32

COLLEGES THAT PROVIDE COURSES IN COMPUTER GRAPHICS AND ANIMATION

TRADITIONAL AND COMPUTER ANIMATION

Algonquin College of Applied Arts and Technology
http://www.algonquinc.on.ca/algweb/index.html

Art Center College of Design
http://www.artcenter.edu/

Art Institute of Chicago
http://www.artic.edu/

Art Institute of Dallas
http://www.aid.aii.edu/

CalArts
http://emsh.calarts.edu/

Cogswell Polytechnical College
http://www.cogswell.edu/FlashSite.html

Mississippi State University (Masters Program)
http://www.msstate.edu/dept/Art/

Ohio State University
http://accad.osu.edu/

Pratt Institute
http://www.pratt.edu/

Rhode Island School of Design
http://www.risd.edu/

Ringling School of Art and Design
http://www.rsad.edu/

San Francisco Academy of Art
http://www.academyart.edu/

San Jose State University
http://www.sjsu.edu/

School of Visual Arts
http://www.sva.edu/

Sheridan College
http://www.sheridanc.on.ca/

Texas A&M University
http://www.tamu.edu/

University of Southern California
http://www.usc.edu/

COMPUTER GRAPHICS

Brown University
http://www.brown.edu/

California State University, East Bay
http://www.csuhayward.edu/

California State University, Irvine
http://www.uci.edu/

California State University, Monterey
http://www.monterey.edu/

Cornell University (Program of Computer Graphics)
http://www.graphics.cornell.edu/

Massachusetts Institute of Technology
http://web.mit.edu/

New York Institute of Technology
http://www.nyit.edu/

Savannah College of Art and Design
http://www.scad.edu

Stanford University (Computer Graphics Laboratory)
http://www-graphics.stanford.edu/

University of California, Berkeley (Computer Science Division)
http://www.cs.berkeley.edu/

University of North Carolina, Chapel Hill (Dept. of Computer Science)
http://www.cs.unc.edu/

University of Pennsylvania
http://www.upenn.edu/

University of Washington (Dept. of Computer Science and Engineering)
http://www.cs.washington.edu/

University of Utah
http://www.utah.edu/

SECTION 34

BOOKS ON VISUAL EFFECTS

The Technique of Special Effects Cinematography
Raymond Fielding
ISBN 0240512340

Special Effects — Wire, Tape and Rubber Band Style
L. B. Abbott
ISBN 0935578064
(This book may be out of print. But if you can find a used copy somewhere it is worth the effort)

Industrial Light & Magic — The Art of Special Effects
Thomas G. Smith
ISBN 0345322630

Industrial Light & Magic — Into the Digital Realm
Mark Cotta Vaz and Patricia Rose Duignan
ISBN 0345381521

Special Effects — The History and Technique
Richard Rickitt
ISBN 0823077330

Photoshop — Studio Secrets
Deke McClelland and Katrin Eismann
ISBN 0764532715
(Chapter 19 is an interview with Eric Chauvin who shows his process for creating digital matte shots)

The Art and Science of Digital Compositing
Ron Brinkmann
ISBN 0121339602

SECTION 35

CONCLUSION

Movies are important. The stories they tell traverse cultures, languages and beliefs. They touch our souls in profound ways, making us laugh, smile and cry. Movies bring adventures that help us see our lives in a different way. They bring knowledge, entertainment and magic into our lives.

Making a movie is a huge endeavor — extremely fulfilling, but also difficult. With today's technology almost anyone can see his dreams light up the big screen. All it takes is passion, time and a little money. Independent films are becoming more important every year as film festivals pop up like mushrooms. Technology brings new opportunities for amateur filmmakers, but sometimes we need a little help. This book will be that guide. Written in plain language, it's simple, yet effective. It isn't meant to be a comprehensive guide to movie special effects, but rather a reference and source of inspiration.

Use the techniques in this book as building blocks to create your own special effects. Try them one at a time, learn how they work, and discover how they can add that elusive **film look** to your next movie. Practice these techniques until you master them. Then, begin adding multiple effects together to create bigger and better scenes. Your imagination is the only limit.

I've been an independent filmmaker for over 12 years. Having learned firsthand how difficult it is to break into Hollywood, I want to educate and support future filmmakers. The field of Special Effects can be a great way to start in the movie business. Special Effects can help launch your career by giving you valuable knowledge and experience, plus the ability to showcase your skill and talent. Remember, there's only one rule for creativity: DON'T GIVE UP.

Passion is a wonderful thing: Do not take it lightly. Your dreams are what make life magical. Fight for them. Be creative. Try new ways of doing things. Go for it!

Have fun, play safe, and enjoy!

Michael Slone

ABOUT THE AUTHOR

Michael Slone has been an independent filmmaker for over 12 years. He has worked on small independent movies, as well as being a part of the major motion picture industry. His titles have included Writer, Director, Producer, Cinematographer, Editor, Soundman and Special Effects Coordinator. He knows how hard it is to break into Hollywood, so he wants to help educate and support future filmmakers in this endeavor. He has collaborated with many different filmmakers on a variety of projects. He finally decided to start his own independent studio, so he created **Studio 7 Productions** in 2002. Filmmaking is one of his greatest passions.

FILM DIRECTING: SHOT BY SHOT

VISUALIZING FROM CONCEPT TO SCREEN

STEVEN D. KATZ

BEST SELLER

OVER 190,000 COPIES SOLD!

Film Directing: Shot by Shot – with its famous blue cover – is the best-known book on directing and a favorite of professional directors as an on-set quick reference guide.

This international bestseller is a complete catalog of visual techniques and their stylistic implications, enabling working filmmakers to expand their knowledge.

Contains in-depth information on shot composition, staging sequences, visualization tools, framing and composition techniques, camera movement, blocking tracking shots, script analysis, and much more.

Includes over 750 storyboards and illustrations, with never-before-published storyboards from Steven Spielberg's *Empire of the Sun*, Orson Welles' *Citizen Kane*, and Alfred Hitchcock's *The Birds*.

"(To become a director) you have to teach yourself what makes movies good and what makes them bad. John Singleton has been my mentor... he's the one who told me what movies to watch and to read Shot by Shot."

- Ice Cube, *New York Times*

"A generous number of photos and superb illustrations accompany each concept, many of the graphics being from Katz' own pen... Film Directing: Shot by Shot *is a feast for the eyes."*

- *Videomaker* Magazine

"... demonstrates the visual techniques of filmmaking by defining the process whereby the director converts storyboards into photographed scenes."

- *Back Stage Shoot*

"Contains an encyclopedic wealth of information."

- *Millimeter* Magazine

STEVEN D. KATZ is also the author of *Film Directing: Cinematic Motion.*

$27.95 · 366 PAGES · ORDER NUMBER 7RLS · ISBN: 0-941188-10-8

24 HOURS | 1.800.833.5738 | WWW.MWP.COM

MICHAEL WIESE PRODUCTIONS

Since 1981, Michael Wiese Productions has been dedicated to providing both novice and seasoned filmmakers with vital information on all aspects of filmmaking. We have published more than 70 books, used in over 500 film schools and countless universities, and by hundreds of thousands of filmmakers worldwide.

Our authors are successful industry professionals who spend innumerable hours writing about the hard stuff: budgeting, financing, directing, marketing, and distribution. They believe that if they share their knowledge and experience with others, more high quality films will be produced.

And that has been our mission, now complemented through our new web-based resources. We invite all readers to visit www.mwp.com to receive free tipsheets and sample chapters, participate in forum discussions, obtain product discounts — and even get the opportunity to receive free books, project consulting, and other services offered by our company.

Our goal is, quite simply, to help you reach your goals. That's why we give our readers the most complete portal for filmmaking knowledge available — in the most convenient manner.

We truly hope that our books and web-based resources will empower you to create enduring films that will last for generations to come.

Let us hear from you at anytime.

Sincerely,

Michael Wiese

Publisher, Filmmaker

www.mwp.com

FILM & VIDEO BOOKS

Cinematic Storytelling: *The 100 Most Powerful Film Conventions Every Filmmaker Must Know* / Jennifer Van Sijll / $24.95

Complete DVD Book, The: *Designing, Producing, and Marketing Your Independent Film on DVD* / Chris Gore and Paul J. Salamoff / $26.95

Complete Independent Movie Marketing Handbook, The: *Promote, Distribute & Sell Your Film or Video* / Mark Steven Bosko / $39.95

Could It Be a Movie?: *How to Get Your Ideas Out of Your Head and Up on the Screen* / Christina Hamlett / $26.95

Creating Characters: *Let Them Whisper Their Secrets*
Marisa D'Vari / $26.95

Crime Writer's Reference Guide, The: *1001 Tips for Writing the Perfect Crime*
Martin Roth / $20.95

Cut by Cut: *Editing Your Film or Video*
Gael Chandler / $35.95

Digital Filmmaking 101, 2nd Edition: *An Essential Guide to Producing Low-Budget Movies* / Dale Newton and John Gaspard / $26.95

Digital Moviemaking, 2nd Edition: *All the Skills, Techniques, and Moxie You'll Need to Turn Your Passion into a Career* / Scott Billups / $26.95

Directing Actors: *Creating Memorable Performances for Film and Television*
Judith Weston / $26.95

Directing Feature Films: *The Creative Collaboration Between Directors, Writers, and Actors* / Mark Travis / $26.95

Eye is Quicker, The: *Film Editing; Making a Good Film Better*
Richard D. Pepperman / $27.95

Fast, Cheap & Under Control: *Lessons Learned from the Greatest Low-Budget Movies of All Time* / John Gaspard / $26.95

Film & Video Budgets, 4th Updated Edition
Deke Simon and Michael Wiese / $26.95

Film Directing: Cinematic Motion, 2nd Edition
Steven D. Katz / $27.95

Film Directing: Shot by Shot, *Visualizing from Concept to Screen*
Steven D. Katz / $27.95

Film Director's Intuition, The: *Script Analysis and Rehearsal Techniques*
Judith Weston / $26.95

Film Production Management 101: *The Ultimate Guide for Film and Television Production Management and Coordination* / Deborah S. Patz / $39.95

Filmmaking for Teens: *Pulling Off Your Shorts*
Troy Lanier and Clay Nichols / $18.95

First Time Director: *How to Make Your Breakthrough Movie*
Gil Bettman / $27.95

From Word to Image: *Storyboarding and the Filmmaking Process*
Marcie Begleiter / $26.95

Hitting Your Mark, 2nd Edition: *Making a Life - and a Living - as a Film Director*
Steve Carlson / $22.95

Hollywood Standard, The: *The Complete and Authoritative Guide to Script Format and Style* / Christopher Riley / $18.95

I Could've Written a Better Movie Than That!: *How to Make Six Figures as a Script Consultant even if You're not a Screenwriter* / Derek Rydall / $26.95

Independent Film Distribution: *How to Make a Successful End Run Around the Big Guys* / Phil Hall / $24.95

Independent Film and Videomakers Guide - 2nd Edition, The: *Expanded and Updated* / Michael Wiese / $29.95

Inner Drives: *How to Write and Create Characters Using the Eight Classic Centers of Motivation* / Pamela Jaye Smith / $26.95

I'll Be in My Trailer!: *The Creative Wars Between Directors & Actors*
John Badham and Craig Modderno / $26.95

Moral Premise, The: *Harnessing Virtue & Vice for Box Office Success*
Stanley D. Williams, Ph.D. / $24.95

Myth and the Movies: *Discovering the Mythic Structure of 50 Unforgettable Films* / Stuart Voytilla / $26.95

On the Edge of a Dream: *Magic and Madness in Bali*
Michael Wiese / $16.95

Perfect Pitch, The: *How to Sell Yourself and Your Movie Idea to Hollywood*
Ken Rotcop / $16.95

Power of Film, The
Howard Suber / $27.95

Psychology for Screenwriters: *Building Conflict in your Script*
William Indick, Ph.D. / $26.95

Save the Cat!: *The Last Book on Screenwriting You'll Ever Need*
Blake Snyder / $19.95

Screenwriting 101: *The Essential Craft of Feature Film Writing*
Neill D. Hicks / $16.95

Screenwriting for Teens: *The 100 Principles of Screenwriting Every Budding Writer Must Know* / Christina Hamlett / $18.95

Script-Selling Game, The: *A Hollywood Insider's Look at Getting Your Script Sold and Produced* / Kathie Fong Yoneda / $16.95

Selling Your Story in 60 Seconds: *The Guaranteed Way to get Your Screenplay or Novel Read* / Michael Hauge / $12.95

Setting Up Your Scenes: *The Inner Workings of Great Films*
Richard D. Pepperman / $24.95

Setting Up Your Shots: *Great Camera Moves Every Filmmaker Should Know*
Jeremy Vineyard / $19.95

Shaking the Money Tree, 2nd Edition: *The Art of Getting Grants and Donations for Film and Video Projects* / Morrie Warshawski / $26.95

Sound Design: *The Expressive Power of Music, Voice, and Sound Effects in Cinema* / David Sonnenschein / $19.95

Stealing Fire From the Gods, 2nd Edition: *The Complete Guide to Story for Writers & Filmmakers* / James Bonnet / $26.95

Storyboarding 101: *A Crash Course in Professional Storyboarding*
James Fraioli / $19.95

Ultimate Filmmaker's Guide to Short Films, The: *Making It Big in Shorts*
Kim Adelman / $16.95

Working Director, The: *How to Arrive, Thrive & Survive in the Director's Chair*
Charles Wilkinson / $22.95

Writer's Journey, - 2nd Edition, The: *Mythic Structure for Writers*
Christopher Vogler / $24.95

Writer's Partner, The: *1001 Breakthrough Ideas to Stimulate Your Imagination*
Martin Roth / $24.95

Writing the Action Adventure: *The Moment of Truth*
Neill D. Hicks / $14.95

Writing the Comedy Film: *Make 'Em Laugh*
Stuart Voytilla and Scott Petri / $14.95

Writing the Killer Treatment: *Selling Your Story Without a Script*
Michael Halperin / $14.95

Writing the Second Act: *Building Conflict and Tension in Your Film Script*
Michael Halperin / $19.95

Writing the Thriller Film: *The Terror Within*
Neill D. Hicks / $14.95

Writing the TV Drama Series: *How to Succeed as a Professional Writer in TV*
Pamela Douglas / $24.95

DVD & VIDEOS

Field of Fish: *VHS Video*
Directed by Steve Tanner and Michael Wiese, Written by Annamaria Murphy / $9.95

Hardware Wars: *DVD* / Written and Directed by Ernie Fosselius / $14.95

Sacred Sites of the Dalai Lamas - DVD, The: *A Pilgrimage to Oracle Lake*
A Documentary by Michael Wiese / $22.95

Food, Community, and the Spirit World

This is a detailed ethnographic study of food beliefs, language, and practices in a rural community of Hassan District, Karnataka State (formerly Mysore), India. The author is an anthropological linguist who resided in the locality for almost two years in 1966-67. He provides the reader with an unusually detailed view of the intersections of language, food, and social relationships. Food is viewed as an important structuring aspect of the Hindu world view, a way that people symbolically represent and reproduce their own identities, gender relationships, and the differences among local castes and sub-castes. The role of foods and food exchange in weddings, ancestor ceremonies, and other family ceremonies is explored. The area studied no longer exists, having been submerged by an irrigation dam project. Includes bibliography and more than 100 photographs.

Review:

Stanley Regelson's Food, Community, and the Spirit World: An Indian Village Study *lives up to its title in many significant ways, by exploring the many meanings and uses of food in different social, religious and historical contexts. Though originally published over fifty years ago, it remains a model for such studies because it presents a wide, highly detailed and linguistically sophisticated picture of the roles of food in these different contexts, based on data collected in a single village. Such detailed studies are very rare.*

FRANKLIN SOUTHWORTH
Professor Emeritus, Linguistics
University of Pennsylvania

ISBN 9780990633785